The Jubilee Years

D1595708

The Jubilee Years

Embracing Clergy Retirement

Bruce G. Epperly

An Alban Institute Book

ROWMAN & LITTLEFIELD
Lanham • Boulder • New York • London

Published by Rowman & Littlefield
An imprint of The Rowman & Littlefield Publishing Group, Inc.
4501 Forbes Boulevard, Suite 200, Lanham, Maryland 20706
www.rowman.com

6 Tinworth Street, London SE11 5AL, United Kingdom

Copyright © 2020 by The Rowman & Littlefield Publishing Group, Inc.

All rights reserved. No part of this book may be reproduced in any form or by any electronic or mechanical means, including information storage and retrieval systems, without written permission from the publisher, except by a reviewer who may quote passages in a review.

British Library Cataloguing in Publication Information Available

Library of Congress Cataloging-in-Publication Data

Names: Epperly, Bruce Gordon, author.
Title: The jubilee years : embracing clergy retirement / Bruce Epperly.
Description: Lanham : Rowman & Littlefield, 2020. | Includes
    bibliographical references and index. | Summary: "Taking inspiration
    from the Spanish word for retirement—jubilación—veteran minister Bruce
    Epperly challenges and empowers clergy to see retirement as a
    celebration of new possibilities and not an inexorable diminishment
    towards irrelevance"— Provided by publisher.
Identifiers: LCCN 2020033385 (print) | LCCN 2020033386 (ebook) | ISBN
    9781538145487 (cloth) | ISBN 9781538145494 (paperback) | ISBN
    9781538145500 (epub)
Subjects: LCSH: Clergy—Retirement.
Classification: LCC BV4382 .E77 2020 (print) | LCC BV4382 (ebook) | DDC
    248.8/92—dc23
LC record available at https://lccn.loc.gov/2020033385
LC ebook record available at https://lccn.loc.gov/2020033386

♾️™ The paper used in this publication meets the minimum requirements of American National Standard for Information Sciences—Permanence of Paper for Printed Library Materials, ANSI/NISO Z39.48-1992.

Contents

A New Beginning

But this I call to mind, and therefore I have hope:
The steadfast love of the LORD never ceases,
God's mercies never come to an end;
they are new every morning;
great is your faithfulness.
"The LORD is my portion," says my soul,
"therefore I will hope in God." (Lamentations 3:21–24, AP)

The words of Lamentations 3 have become my spiritual anchor as I look toward the challenges of spiritual growth during retirement. Through all the anticipated changes of life, professional, personal, and relational, these words affirm that God is faithful. As the apostle Paul proclaims, nothing in all creation—including aging and death—"will be able to separate us from the love of God in Christ Jesus" (Romans 8:39). This is the hope to which I cling as I gaze at the horizons of retirement with full awareness that the years ahead will bring expected and unexpected changes in body, mind, and spirit as well as in my personal vocation and professional life.

In my late sixties, I am looking for wisdom to guide me on the pathway ahead. Although I am still active and plan to remain active in ministry, writing, and academic life, the coming of every day brings reminders of my mortality and the realities of the aging process. Life is all too brief, yet also amazing and adventurous. I anticipate many more years of creativity and adventure, and daily I ask myself, in the spirit of poet Mary Oliver's "Summer Day," what do I intend to do with my unique, precious, and wonderful life? Although I cannot control my personal and professional future in their entirety and must face the possibility of debilitation in mind, body, and spirit, I want to be among those who experience life in all its abundance for the next few decades and hopefully to the very end. Like most people, I want to be active and generative, making a difference to my wife, son, daughter-in-law, and grandchildren, faith community, and larger Christian and non-Christian communities. I want to teach and write for as long as I have breath. I want to continue my quest for justice and planetary healing in my personal and vocational life even beyond my official retirement.

It was quite synchronous that I came upon an announcement for the Louisville Institute's Pastoral Study Program. Nearly a decade before, I received a Louisville Institute grant to study best spiritual and professional practices for new ministers making the transition from seminary to their first congregational call. That yearlong study eventuated in the publication of *Starting with Spirit: Nurturing Your Call to Pastoral Leadership.*[1] It seemed appropriate at this time of my life to embark on a study of the experiences of retired clergy as a way of integrating my professional commitment to serve the church and its clergy with my personal quest for wholeness and generativity in the decades to come.

Over a yearlong period, I conversed with nearly a hundred pastors, one to one in coffee houses, restaurants, and living rooms; I met with retired clergy groups and conducted phone interviews. I traveled coast to coast in the United States and north to Canada to meet with retired clergy from a variety of denominations. My goal was to listen to pastors sharing their retirement experiences. I wanted to hear their challenges, joys, hopes, and fears. I was interested in discovering what gets them up in the morning looking forward to a new day. I wanted to discover how clergy prepared for retirement and what activities and values shaped their lives in retirement.

While retirement brings significant personal and professional changes, I believe that retired clergy can be transformational leaders. No longer tethered to the politics and administrative duties of congregational leadership, they can now freely commit themselves to spiritual growth and community and planetary healing and transformation. Retired clergy can become sages and wisdom givers, sharing their insights and energy with congregations and communities.

While my approach was ambient and anecdotal rather than analytic and ethnographic in the narrow sense of the word, I sought to interview persons from diverse denominations, theological perspectives, and ethnic and racial backgrounds. Although I attempted to be as diverse as possible in my conversations, trying to go beyond my own social and theological location, my interviews nevertheless reflected my own religious and personal communities—primarily Caucasian and theologically progressive, mainstream Protestant. I decided at the outset to report the conversations in this book pseudonymously, except those conversations with retired clergy whose professional and public work was well known and could easily be identified. I also focused on interviewing Protestant Christians. In terms of gender and sexual identity, about 60 percent of my interviews involved cisgender men. I also met with a handful of persons of color and several retired clergy from the LGBTQ+ community. This, in part, reflects the demographics of retired clergy, which will be quite different ten years from now.

I expected to encounter women and men of stature, and my expectations were exceeded. Virtually all the pastors with whom I spoke are committed to spiritual and intellectual growth, exploring new possibilities and making a difference in our planet's future. All of them connected their well-being with the future health of their communities and the planet and were committed to being as active as possible joining local and global concern. Freed from congregational limitations, most of them embodied the call to move from self-interest to world loyalty. Many saw the final decades of life as an opportunity to deepen their spirituality and come to know God face to face in the spirit of the mystical tradition, while remaining active in the hardscrabble world of public affairs and politics. The majority also saw retirement as a time to explore interests they had deferred because of their commitments to full-time ministry. Family life and personal gifts, often crowded out by ministerial demands, now were center stage, especially in terms of nurturing grandchildren, spending time with spouses, and exploring new gifts, talents, and mission opportunities. I was inspired by their desire to keep the faith regardless of their health condition as well as their recognition that vocation does not end with retirement but takes new and creative shapes when liberated from institutional constraints.

My conversations with pastors joined the theological, spiritual, and practical aspects of personal and professional life and gave shape to my reflections. In the course of this text, I will be integrating the stories of retired pastors with theological reflections and spiritual practices to nurture your own preparation for retirement or enrich your current life situation as retired clergy. As you read these words, my hope is that you will look forward to your own retirement as a holy adventure, embodying our vocation to be God's companions in healing the world. If you are retired, I hope these words will inspire new and adventurous pathways of service, family life, and creativity.

I am grateful to the Louisville Institute and its superlative and supportive leadership team—Edwin Aponte, Don Richter, Pam Collins, and Keri Lietchty. I am also grateful to the recipients of 2019 Pastoral Study Project grants whose comments enlivened my work. As always, I am grateful to my very active and supportive in-house "retired" clergy person, Kate Epperly, and to my son Matt and daughter-in-law Ingrid and my grandchildren Jack and James, whose presence enlivens my days and inspires my quest to heal the earth for future generations of God's beloved human and nonhuman children. I am grateful to the congregations and institutions that nurtured my professional life, especially what I anticipate being my final full-time congregation, South Congregational Church, United Church of Christ, Centerville, Massachusetts. This Cape Cod village church has encouraged my creativity through sabbatical and research time as well as their support of my academic and literary pursuits.

It is my prayer that as you read this, your own retirement or your relationships with retired clergy will be blessed and inspired. It is my hope that you will see retirement as an opportunity for growth and adventure as you seek to be God's companion in healing the planet one day at a time and all the days of your life.

NOTE

1. Bruce Epperly, *Starting with Spirit: Nurturing Your Call to Pastoral Leadership* (Lanham, MD: Rowman & Littlefield, 2010).

Chapter 1

Invitation to Adventure

For all that has been—thanks!
For all that shall be—yes![1]

At a recent Louisville Institute Pastoral Study Program seminar, one of the participants responded to my presentation on clergy retirement with a provocative definition of the word "retirement." "The word for retirement in Spanish is 'jubilacion' like the English word jubilation or joy!" she noted. Her comment astonished and awakened me to a new way of looking at retirement. When seen as a Jubilee, new and positive dimensions of retirement emerge. No longer do we view retirement as a time of slowing down, letting go, and absenting ourselves from the maelstrom of social involvement. Retirement is a Jubilee, a harvest celebration, an affirmation of life, a time of joy and commemoration, and an opportunity for new adventures. It may even involve, as the biblical Jubilee year counsels, personal reorientation and the discovery of new values and vocations. Retirement may involve retrospection and introspection and turning inward. It may also involve transformation, forward movement, creativity, and action. In the Jubilee years, we give thanks for what has been. We also let go of the past to go forward and say "yes" to new life.

As I pondered my colleague's comment, my thoughts went to the biblical notion of the Jubilee Year (Leviticus 25:8–12), proposed as a time of social and personal transformation, to occur every fifty years.

> You shall count off seven weeks of years, seven times seven years, so that the period of seven weeks of years gives forty-nine years. Then you shall have the trumpet sounded loud; on the tenth day of the seventh month—on the day of atonement—you shall have the trumpet sounded throughout all your land. And

1

you shall hallow the fiftieth year and you shall proclaim liberty throughout the land to all its inhabitants. It shall be a jubilee for you: you shall return, every one of you, to your property and every one of you to your family. That fiftieth year shall be a jubilee for you: you shall not sow, or reap the aftergrowth, or harvest the unpruned vines. For it is a jubilee; it shall be holy to you: you shall eat only what the field itself produces.

Imagine retirement as a Jubilee Year of holiness and harvest, of making amends and letting go of the past, and then moving forward, traveling light on a holy adventure. Imagine not just one year but, perhaps, two or three decades of Jubilee Years, devoted to playing your emerging role in healing the world and embodying the spirit of Shalom in your daily life. Relieved of the responsibilities of full-time ministerial employment or the need to conform to others' expectations, retired pastors can proclaim a Jubilee, healing the past and transforming the future, the inner journey of introspection giving birth to inspiring service in the world.

Retirement is a time of liberation, a season involving the interplay of freedom from previous commitments and freedom for personal and social transformation. Now we have time for the things we left undone as a result of busy ministerial schedules. Now can explore new pathways and parts of ourselves we have neglected as a result of professional ambitions and demands.

I began working on this project on clergy retirement the year I became a member of the Medicare generation. A decade earlier, in my mid-fifties, I penned a book aimed at providing guidance for recently ordained pastors, making the transition from seminary to their first ministerial calls.[2] I reflected with these newly minted pastors on the "firsts" of ministry—first call, first sermon, first death, first memorial service, first wedding, and first baptism. At the edges of their promised lands, looking toward new horizons of ministry, I noted that they would have many adventures and see many strange beasts. In my conversation with new pastors, I presented a vision of healthy and successful ministry, embracing a whole-person spirituality that joined the inner and outer journeys to deepen and undergird our ministries.

Now, on the edge of my own retirement, I pondered another promised land with its own new horizons. As I conversed with retired pastors, I found myself contemplating the dynamics of a pastor's "exit" from full-time ministry, knowing that in the next five years or so, I will be taking this journey myself. In the spirit of the Jubilee Year, many pastors have reached the fifty-year milestone of ministry, the trajectory beginning with their call to ministry, later seminary and the ordination process, and extending over four decades. While some of their companions began the ministerial adventure in midlife, both groups are on the verge of experiencing the "lasts" of ministry—last full-time congregation, last confirmation class, last baptism, last annual congregational meeting, last stewardship campaign, last sermon, last memorial service, last wedding, and the last farewell. Some may ease out of full-time ministry through interim ministry or part-time small church or specialized ministry, but even in embarking on these new projects they are on the edge of another promised land, knowing that they must take the journey through the wilderness of professional and spiritual redefinition and transformation.

Just as new pastors are counseled to "start with spirit," pastors considering or beginning retirement can also begin their new journeys, guided by God's Spirit and intentionally nurturing spiritual gifts appropriate to the next stages of their pilgrimage. They can see retirement as Jubilee not withdrawal and as the womb possibility not the prison house of limitation.

For the past several years, I have begun each day with the affirmation "This is the day that God has made. I will rejoice and be glad in it!" (Psalm 118:24). As I consider my own aging and retirement, both of which shape my present and future planning, the commitment to live each day fully has become the heart of my spirituality. Each moment is precious and an opportunity to incarnate the sacrament of the present moment. I have discovered that retirement is not just about concluding my professional life sometime in the future. It also involves the decisions I make today. I am creating my retirement by the quality of my personal choices in the areas of health, finances, relationships, learning, politics, and spirituality. In this Holy Moment, the future emerges out of our past and present decisions. The call of retirement involves imagining a creative future while seeking excellence in my vocation today.

Retirement is ultimately a spiritual and theological issue for clergy and laypersons alike. While we cannot fully determine the events that shape our lives, our attitudes, as Viktor Frankl asserts, are in our hands and give shape to the apparently unchosen and random events of life. We can lose everything and still be faithful to God's vision for our lives and the world. We can jettison our professional identity of fifty years and midwife new creativity and commitment and new ways to describe ourselves. Our vision of reality can promote hopefulness or hopelessness as we face the future. Our spiritual practices can guide the moral and professional arc of our lives well beyond our final days of employment. In every transitional time from first congregational call to retirement, we need vital and living theologies, expressed in healthy spiritual practices, to enable us to have, in the words of the hymn, Great Is Thy Faithfulness:

strength for today and bright hope for tomorrow,
blessings all mine and ten thousand beside.

Depending on our attitude to the planned and unplanned events of our lives, retirement can be apocalyptic or adventurous. When we let go of a lifetime of professional practices that have defined who we are, focused our daily attention, constituted our relationships, and shaped our spirituality, we are confronted with the great, "What's next?" Pondering his mortality, Leo Tolstoy's Ivan Ilych queries, "What I be when I am no more?" While retirement is not necessarily the prelude to death, leaving our accustomed habits and habitats evokes the same concerns. We must die to the familiar to be born to new possibilities. We ask in the words of many of the pastors I interviewed:

> Who will I be when I am no longer a professional minister? How will I introduce myself when meeting new people? How will my change in professional status alter my relationships, many of which have been with congregants and fellow pastors? Will I be viewed as a source of wisdom or seen as irrelevant, left behind by the changes in demographics and congregational life? Will fellow judicatory officials and fellow pastors, especially my successor in the congregation I'm currently leading, view me as a threat or nuisance, someone to be admonished, like a newcomer to ministry, on the importance of clergy boundaries, or will they see me as the source of wisdom, born of a lifetime of study, commitment, and experience?

Worse yet, as I and other pastors look at our own lives, "Will I become one of those intrusive 'old farts' who need to comment on everything and insert themselves where they don't belong? Will I doubt my value to the larger community or see myself as providing nothing of use to my colleagues, congregation, and newcomers to ministry?"

No doubt the parents of the Abrahamic religions, Sarai and Abram, asked their own version of these questions when God called them from the comforts of retirement to journey to an unknown land, without providing a map or directions. They had to let go of their previous social standing and identity to embrace God's new possibilities for them. I suspect that they did not answer the call to move on immediately, but considered their personal, financial, and relational resources for the journey. Relentless though God's call was, they crunched the numbers, made financial preparations, adjusted plans, and imagined a future without the activities and vocations that previously defined their lives. Little did they know that the journey would be filled with conflict and uncertainty. What they could not yet imagine was that they would have encounters with angels and would discover a new land, rejoice at the birth of a child, and receive new names reflective of their changed spiritual status.

Going forth from the familiarities of ministry, we may also have unexpected adventures, face peril, and encounter angelic strangers. We will not be alone on our pilgrimage. We will be accompanied by a generation of baby boomers and their elders, retiring or preparing for retirement, fellow companions on the Way of Jubilee. Like Sarai and Abram, we will pilgrim in companionship with God and in the process receive new names and responsibilities commensurate with our experience and imagination.

The adventure of retirement involves the interplay of "thanks" and "yes" and gratitude and intentionality. Our sense of gratitude and hope for the future are profoundly theological and spiritual in nature. Gratitude is an affirmation of the dynamic and graceful interdependence of life. When the apostle Paul counsels the Philippians, "Do not worry about anything, but in everything by prayer and supplication with thanksgiving, let your requests be made known to God" (Philippians 4:6), he is inviting us to see our lives as part of a larger story, encompassing our relationships, institutions, culture, and planetary environment, undergirded and permeated by the graceful providence of God. No one succeeds on their own. Our lives emerge out of an intricate and supportive divine environment, reflecting divine wisdom and compassion throughout every season. Although imprisoned, the apostle Paul can look back gratefully on God's quiet, and occasionally dramatic, presence in his family of origin, religious and educational training, mystical experiences, and supportive relationships in the Philippian community.

In the spirit of the apostle Paul, an American Baptist pastor with whom I spoke described his ministry of forty-two years in the words of the hymn "Amazing Grace." He averred,

> At this point, I give thanks for the whole journey, good times and tough times. I can confidently say, "Through many dangers toils and snares I have already come. Tis grace has brought me safe thus far and grace will lead me home." I've had some challenges and conflicts professionally and they've left scars on my personal and professional life, but God has been with me, and by facing these with God and my family, I have grown spiritually and this has made all the difference in my ministry, marriage, parenting, and now grandparenting.

"God is near," Paul affirms (Philippians 4:5). For those pastors who cultivate a sense of intimacy with God through prayer, study, contemplation, and relationships, ministry embodies the "sacrament of the present moment," as Pierre de Caussade claims, in which a personal and intimate God addresses us in the ordinary and dramatic events of our lives. A spirituality of gratitude is grounded in a theology of relationship with God and the world. Looking back on nearly four decades of rural and small-town ministry, a Midwest United Methodist pastor confesses,

> I feel like the character in the poem "Footprints." In those moments, when I thought I was alone and on my own, God was carrying me. God was bringing

persons into my life whose wisdom kept me honest and faithful in ministry. I never thought I would spend my whole life in rural and small-town churches. When I left seminary, I wanted the excitement of the city. I wanted to confront the powers and principalities at work in poverty, racism, and addiction. To my surprise, I found out that I could be change agent in rural America, too, responding to the hidden realities of hopelessness and substance use disorder. I also had to change my attitudes to sink deep roots in the community. I found a way to mate my progressive theology and politics with my moderately conservative congregations. My children are now grown up with families of their own, but they often comment on the values they received in the small towns where I pastored—a father who attended every game and was available when they needed him, safe streets, and a sense of place.

As he reflects on what is to come, having relocated to a county seat town, thirty miles from his last congregation, he notes, "I am so thankful and while I still have energy I want to make a difference in this town of 15,000. I want to use my skills in connecting and communication to help improve the lives of people here. God is carrying me still." For all that has been in the ups and downs of our lives and ministries, let us give thanks!

The great "yes" of life and ministry arises from a sense of an open future in which our decisions can make a difference. I believe our task in life is to be God's companions in healing the world one moment and one action at a time. In the spirit of Jewish mysticism, I affirm that when you save a soul, you save the world. When we bring beauty and wholeness to a moment or an encounter, we push forward the arc of justice. Healthy retirement can involve the gift of a theological vision in which new possibilities loom on the horizon. Despite the past, each moment can be an opportunity for creative transformation embodied in choices that open our hearts, hands, and heads. Retirement is an end, and it is also a new beginning. As Paul advises the Christians at Rome, "Do not be conformed to this world but be transformed by the renewing of your minds, so that you may discern what is the will of God—what is good and acceptable and perfect" (Romans 12:2).

Invoking the specter of retirement often places limits on us, based on social stereotypes related to aging, productivity, and work. The happiest retired pastors shake off these limits and create new forms of retirement as their lives unfold. As a Minnesota United Church of Christ pastor noted, "Once I was fixated on the ministry of the church where I was called to pastor. Now that I am retired, I feel like John Wesley. My parish is the world. Not tethered to an institution, I have become a rabble rouser, challenging our governmental and business leaders' complacency about global climate change. I no longer worry about next year's budget. I am concerned with the health of the next several generations of humans and the nonhuman world with whom we share the planet."

Her ministry has expanded from church loyalty to world loyalty. She knows that the future is, in good measure, in our hands as well as God's. God has not written the final story line for planet Earth. Recognizing that the future is open for her and the planet, she does her part to be, in her words, "a co-creator with God in ensuring the survival of the planet." For this retired pastor, hope in the future spurs her to ecological activism. As she looks at the harsh realities of climate change, she is filled with the fierce urgency of hope for the future. She knows that the future of the planet is uncertain and that our business and political leaders are stoking the fires of planetary destruction, focusing on short-term profit instead of long-term sustainability. But she is doing her part. "Whether or not my efforts are successful in healing the planet, I must be faithful to God's call." She has discovered that a hopeful retirement joins an affirmation of God's presence in the past and God's inspiration for the future. Once again, with the author of Lamentations 2:22–4, we can give thanks and find hope in the interplay of God's faithful presence and God's restless spirit, incarnate in the future that lies ahead for us:

> The steadfast love of God never ceases, his mercies never come to an end; they are new every morning; great is your faithfulness. "The Lord is my portion," says my soul. "therefore I will hope in him."

In the chapters ahead, we will explore how retirement can be the open door to spiritual, relational, and social transformation. We will hear the stories of retired pastors, reflect on spiritual practices that enhance our sense of vocation in retirement, and look at practical behaviors that promote personal wholeness and service to the community, and theological visions that inspire transformation in every season of life. I will share my own retirement reflections in conversation with those pastors who are further along the trail of retirement than myself. I will also wrestle with my own questions and concerns as I listen to their wisdom, charting my own vision quest in tandem with the pilgrim journeys of other pastors and the growing need for retired pastors to become God's partners in healing the world. The vague outlines of retirement are becoming more visible for me with each day and I pray that when I finally embark on the journey, whether by choice or necessity, I will carry these pastors' insights, affirmations, and cautions with me in my own Jubilee years.

PATHWAYS TO JUBILEE

Ministers are the spiritual children of the prophets, healers, and shamans. As pastors, we are, as Marcus Borg notes, spirit persons, whose attention to the

Holy enables us to be companions in mediating spiritual experiences to others. Every aspect of ministry has a spiritual component, just as all life is holy. Our best ministry occurs when we join the inner and outer journeys of faith, integrating prayer and meditation with social concern and organizational effectiveness.

As we prepare for retirement, we need to cultivate holistic theological visions and spiritual practices to serve as guideposts for the journey of retirement, inspiring Jubilee rather than regret. In times of transition, theological reflection and spiritual practice become more important in orienting our spiritual GPS toward new horizons. Each chapter will include a theologically grounded spiritual practice to support your journey toward healthy and transformational retirement.

An Attitude of Gratitude

The affirmation "For all that has been—thanks! For all that shall be—yes!" is at the heart of the Jubilee years. Gratitude connects us with the graceful interdependence of life and reminds us of the blessings that have led to our current life situation. Despite the challenges of ministry and retirement, we can say "thanks" to the Giver, the gifts, and those persons and situations that have undergirded our spiritual journey. From grateful recognition of all that is good, we can accept the imperfections of our lives and ministries and seek to change what we can as we look toward the future. Grounded in gratitude, we can open to the great "yes" of what shall be, actively seeking to be God's companions in healing the world.

For what are you thankful? Find a quiet place for reflection, whether in your study or on a scenic walk. Visualize the many blessings you have received in your ministerial journey. Who were the pivotal persons in your personal and spiritual formation? Who were you teachers, whether lay, academic, or ministerial? What were the moments of grace? At some point, pause for a few minutes to "count your blessings," past and present, writing them down as you reflect on your professional and personal journey. Take some time for prayers of gratitude to the ever-present, always faithful God.

Visualizing Your Future

Grounded in gratitude, open your imagination to the great "yes" that lies ahead of you. Visualize yourself as a pilgrim on a never-ending journey. Where is your journey taking you? What images and possibilities lure you forward? What paths might take you toward the "promised lands" that await you? Take some time for prayers of affirmation for all that will be as you sojourn with God as your companion and guide.

A Prayer for the Pathway. Giver of all good gifts, thank you for the blessings I have received. Thank you for loved ones, friends, family, mentors, and companions on the journey. Thank you for moments of insight as well as moments of caution. Let me always be grateful.

Holy One, open my heart to possibility. Let me have the courage to venture into untraveled lands and the insight to search for paths of wholeness and service. Bless my pilgrimage and bless the journeys of my friends in ministry. In God's loving name. Amen.

NOTES

1. Dag Hammarskjold, *Markings* (New York: Knopf, 1964), 89.
2. Bruce Epperly, *Starting with Spirit: Nurturing Your Call to Pastoral Leadership* (Lanham, MD: Rowman & Littlefield, 2010).

Chapter 2

Theological Guideposts

Do not be conformed to this world, but be transformed by the renewing of your minds, so that you may discern what is the will of God—what is good and acceptable and perfect. (Romans 12:2)

As I was winding down my conversation with my friend of nearly four decades George Hermanson, a retired United Church of Canada pastor and veteran of forty years in college, congregational, and retreat ministries, George offered a piece of advice for pastors considering retirement: "Get a theology. My theology has enabled me to see retirement as a time of possibility and hope. Without a theology, you don't have a roadmap for the adventure ahead."[1]

Dan, a United Church of Christ pastor, now living in Virginia, recalls his spiritual director advising him to place "thinking theologically" at the heart of his ministry. His spiritual director believed that good theology complemented spiritual practices and provided a lens through which to view the expected and unexpected events of life. This advice guided Dan through the ups and downs of over twenty years of ministry and inspired his advocacy for persons with disabilities across his denomination. His theology also served as a polestar for his final, conflict-ridden, ministerial call, reminding him that there is more to life than congregational ministry and opening him to new possibilities for service to the wider community. Dan describes his theology as more experiential than doctrinal. He finds God more in relationships than in creeds. For Dan, theology constantly invites him to ask, "Where is God in all of this?" and given the current chaos of U.S. politics, "What is the work God calls me to do?" These questions have led Dan to pursue political activism and social justice in his retirement. Dan notes that his commitment to practical theology has alerted him to the importance of transforming our political system by "getting big money out of politics so the real needs of the people can be served, not just the prerogatives of corporations and the wealthiest 1%."

Recognizing God's presence in the unplanned events of our lives, much to his surprise, Dan chose to become the co-pastor of a new church start, a progressive Christian voice in the conservative religious Bible Belt of Virginia. "I had not imagined leading a congregation again, but I felt the call to help revive this small, but lively community of faith." For Dan, theology is profoundly concrete, emerging out of the pain and challenges of daily life, and not abstract creedal pronouncements, applicable to everyone, yet relevant to no one! Dan embodies the spirit of H. Richard Niebuhr's responsive ethics: "God is acting in all actions upon you. So respond to all actions upon you as to respond to his action."[2]

Anna, who has also served over four decades both as a congregational pastor and conference minister in the United Church Christ, noted the importance of theology as she lives into retirement. Like Dag Hammarskjold, she interprets the world through the theological lenses of gratitude and providence, despite having experienced some of the limitations of the aging process. "I am filled with gratitude that I still have opportunities to use my skills and gifts—when I feel like saying yes to invitations, such as supply preaching. And in retirement, I experience a deeper sense of God's continuity; I'll be gone but the work will live on." She finds consolation in God's faithfulness in all the seasons of life and God's preservation of all that is good. She finds hope in what Hammarskjold called the "yes" of a future, that is, in her own words, treasured by God "for whom none of our efforts and accomplishments are lost but are preserved as contributions to God's ongoing care for the world." Regardless of what the future brings, she believes that "God will provide us with the resources we need to respond faithfully and lovingly to the events of personal and political lives."

Shaped by process theology, Susan, a Northern California United Methodist pastor is devoting her retirement to responding to the threats exacerbated by global climate change. "We live in an interdependent world in which everything we do matters. The future is wide open, even for God, and God needs us to be co-creators of a positive future." Moreover, she notes that "the non-human world is also loved by God. The whole world is alive with experience and that means that I must do all I can to prevent the suffering and extinction of non-human species, regardless of human interests." Susan spends much of her retirement free time as a resource in climate change for congregations, regularly calls her representatives, and advocates for strict environmental regulations. "The future is at stake, and what I do matters. I want to be faithful to God in my stewardship of the planet and my daily life."

Ken's retirement journey was inspired by the title of Francis Schaffer's book, "How Then, Shall We Live?" After taking a six-month hiatus from any church involvement, in which he regularly asked himself "How Shall I Live?" this retired Presbyterian minister experienced God's guidance to become active in fundraising for various organizations, ranging from congregational capital campaigns to feeding programs for persons experiencing homelessness and school scholarships for children in Southern Sudan. Ken is motivated by a theology of generosity, challenging those who have blessed by financial largesse to share their blessings with persons experiencing poverty and injustice.

My graduate school classmate, Ignacio Castuera, who has spent nearly a half century in congregational and connectional ministries of the United Methodist Church, stated, "My whole ministry has been shaped by process and liberation theology.[3] I have continued and expanded this in retirement. I am blessed to be living in Claremont, California, where I can work regularly with John Cobb, one of our professors and the most influential voice in process theology."

Ignacio often accompanies process theologian John Cobb, who was ninety-four when I interviewed Ignacio in 2019, on his national and global travels and averred that the two of them are planning a trip to Brazil, where the venerable Cobb will be lecturing. Together, Cobb and Castuera have traveled to China, South America, and Europe to share the practical applications of process theology. These days, Ignacio is actively involved in political activism related to ecology and social justice.

Charlie, a retired Southern Baptist pastor, now residing in Southern California, sees the power of God's promises as central to his retirement and aging process. "Scripture provides the guidepost for the road I must travel. I take comfort in God's promise that whether I live or die, I belong to God. I lean on Paul's witness that nothing can separate me from the love of God. This has helped me face my own and my wife's ongoing chronic illnesses and my own aging process with a sense of hope. I can't do as much as I used to at my church or in working with the poor, but I can still pray. When I volunteer at our church's soup kitchen ministry, I pray for everyone going down the line. I believe prayer changes things."

Despite their theological and political differences, Charlie's theology mirrors that of Roman Catholic mystic and social activist Dorothy Day, who, after she was sidelined with ill-health in her seventies, devoted her days to prayer. She discovered that even if she could not picket, she could still pray that God's will be done on earth as it is in heaven. Both Charlie and Dorothy Day believe that prayer makes a difference in the lives of persons and institutions and that our prayers help shape the future in ways we can never fully predict or imagine. Charlie notes that in retirement he has made a commitment to exploring new forms of prayer, including silent meditation and meditating with icons, and this has changed my perspective. When I was actively involved in ministry in Southern Baptist churches, I was clear about my doctrinal positions regarding God's nature, the scope of salvation, and what it means to be saved. It was mostly words, I confess. Time for truly contemplative prayer, for going into the Garden where Jesus "walks with me and talks with me" has widened my perspective. God is bigger than the conservative theology and politics I preached from the pulpit. I still struggle with some of the religious flash point issues like gay marriage, but I no longer condemn people of different beliefs and lifestyles nor do I think my way is the only way to God. I have come to accept gay and lesbians and persons of other faiths as God's children, too. That has been one of the most significant changes during retirement, and some of it is due to being freed from my denomination's theological constraints. In silent prayer, I have come to experience a sense of unity with Christians from other denominations and people from other religions.

While more conservative than most of the retired clergy with whom I spoke, Charlie's evangelical faith embodies the universalizing stage of faith, described by James Fowler. Unlike many of his evangelical companions, his spiritual and theological growth has taken him beyond nation-first and church-first ideologies to world loyalty.

THEOLOGICAL RESOURCES FOR CREATIVE TRANSFORMATION

For many years, I have reminded my seminary students and fellow pastors that they are the primary theologians of the congregations. I tell them that even if they have a well-known seminary professor or author in their congregation, they are the ones, who by their weekly teaching, preaching, and worship leadership, set the theological tone of their congregations. Moreover, I challenge seminarians and pastors to develop well-thought-out and flexible theological positions to shape not only their preaching but also their social involvement and congregational leadership. A well-articulated theological viewpoint, along with personal maturity, awareness of congregational systems theory, and good communication skills, enables the pastor to face congregational conflict and crisis from a perspective beyond self-interest and professional survival. Theology places our lives in a larger story in which divine guidance and providential support is present even in the most challenging events of personal and professional life.

During a time in which my professional integrity was questioned, I found consolation and courage in remembering that God is "the fellow sufferer who understands," as the philosopher Alfred North Whitehead asserts, and that even in the most conflictual situations, God is presenting me with possibilities and the energy to achieve them. Regardless of what the future may bring, God can help us discover a way when, first, we believed there was no path forward.

Although theology is often underestimated as we focus on the practical necessities of retirement, most especially finances, living arrangements, and health concerns, theology matters! Theology provides light on our pathway and enables us to face life's challenges with hope and grace. Theology helps us respond to new possibilities along with the necessary losses and "unfixables" of the aging process.[4]

My own theology of ministry and retirement has been shaped by the process theology, inspired by Alfred North Whitehead and articulated by John Cobb, Bernard Loomer, and David Griffin, and the influence of Christian mystics such as Howard Thurman, Julian of Norwich, and Pierre de Caussade, along with the theological spirituality of Celtic Christian tradition. As I look toward my own retirement, I am guided by the following affirmations of faith.

The Future Is Wide Open and Invites Us to Explore New Possibilities

In describing God's relationship with the world, the author of Lamentations poetically proclaims:

The steadfast love of the LORD never ceases,
    God's mercies never come to an end;
they are new every morning;
    great is your faithfulness. (Lamentations 3:22–23, NRSV, AP)

This affirmation has guided my personal and professional life for four decades. It is a recurring mantra in this book and my personal adventure. When my son was diagnosed with cancer, initially I had no words for prayer except the Jesus' prayer, "Lord, have mercy. Christ, have mercy. Lord, have mercy." When treatment began, I felt a ray of hope that God was with us and that regardless of what the future would bring, God would provide a healing path. I began to sing, "Great is Thy Faithfulness," as I walked the hospital grounds as a reminder that God is with us and that God's vision will guide our decisions and undergird our hopes for the future.

Great is Thy faithfulness! Great is Thy faithfulness!
    Morning by morning new mercies I see;
All I have needed Thy hand hath provided—
    Great is Thy faithfulness, Lord, unto me!

As I look toward my own retirement and all the changes that will occur as I will be forced to redefine my professional and personal life, I am inspired by the affirmation that the future is open, and that God is constantly doing a new thing and inviting me to be part of God's new world, personally and relationally. The book of life is open-ended. The past is significant in shaping the present and future. But in the Holy Here and Now, we have freedom to choose new pathways and embrace new identities. Not bound by predestination or determinism, God and humankind move forward toward the open-ended vision of Shalom. We are shaping the present and future as we go along. In this present moment, God is providing me with short-term and long-term possibilities to embody in my own unique way, given my life experiences, history, gifts, and context. I do not need to recreate the past nor am I doomed to repeat the same behaviors in the future. I can choose to embrace novelty and explore new versions of myself. The open-endedness of the future inspires retired pastors to focus on new talents and embrace new adventures. Recognizing that the future is open and that our actions make a difference, many retired pastors commit themselves to becoming God's partners in healing the world.

Reflecting on her own theological resources, Susan notes, "When I see what our government and industry is doing in terms of incarcerating children at the borders, rolling back protections of the LGBTQ community and women, and contributing to environmental destruction, I am tempted to give up hope. Then, I realize that there can be an alternative future and that I can play a role in it. What I do can make a difference for future generations. And so, I picket and protest. I agitate for a better future for future generations of humans and other species."

Susan's recognition that she can help shape the future has inspired her to go from self-interest to world loyalty. As I ponder the growing ecological consciousness of many retired pastors, who have recognized that there is no time to waste in responding to human-caused climate change, I recall the words of Rabbi Hillel:

If I am not for myself, who will be for me?
If I am not for others, what am I?
And if not now, when?

While these pastors still know how to have a good time as grandparents, folk musicians, artists, athletes, writers, theater goers, and global travelers, their recognition that they can make a difference the world's future has widened their vision from self-interest to world loyalty. In the words of Mother Teresa, Saint Teresa, of Calcutta, they want to do something beautiful for God. They know that bringing beauty to the world requires us to embrace perspectives that ensure the well-being of future generations and persons we will never meet.

The openness of the future energizes me as I ponder my own retirement. While sometime in the future I will miss regular opportunities preaching, adult faith formation classes at church, and sharing in the joys and sorrows of my congregants' lives, I know that God still has a vision for my life and that I can choose new pathways, grounded in over forty years of study and ministry.

Joining Tradition and Novelty

God's relationship to the world and humankind involves the dynamic interplay of stability and change and tradition and novelty. A God worthy of our trust must be faithful and loving. The character of God's love must be unchanging, while adapting to each new moment of experience. A God with whom we can relate must also be intimate, dynamic, and innovative, responding moment to our deepest needs and providentially moving through our lives and the world.

The philosopher Alfred North Whitehead, whose metaphysical vision is fundamental for process theologians like myself, invoked the hymn "Abide with Me" as definitive of the nature of reality:

Abide with me.
Fast falls the eventide.

Permanence and tradition, and the gifts of the past are essential for a good life. But life changes and we must creatively respond, initiating novelty to match the novelties of our lives. God is doing a new thing and we need to align ourselves with God's emerging visions for us and the world.

The reality of retirement changes everything. Sharon, a Central Pennsylvania United Methodist pastor, recalls initially feeling disoriented following her retirement. When she began visiting nearby churches in her denomination, she felt like a "nobody, without any status or role. Someone else was stage managing the service and sharing God's word with the congregation." Sharon confesses that "it took a while for me to claim my place as a 'layperson' without authority in the church, despite the fact that the pastor honored my ordination and gifts." Several months later, Sharon is reclaiming her pastoral mantle as the leader of a midweek Bible study at the church she has chosen to attend. Now that she has reclaimed the identity of "congregant with ministerial credentials," she is grateful that the congregation's pastor trusts her to share her scholarship with the congregation. She is also drawing on her past experiences as a pastor and the theological principles that shaped her life and ministry. "I understand the Apostles Creed differently now than I used to. But

I still recite it daily as my spiritual anchor. My ideas about God have changed but God is still the Maker of Heaven and Earth and I trust in the resurrection of the dead and life everlasting through all the changes I am facing."

Sharon feels liberated from the task of weekly preaching. Still enjoying sermon preparation and wanting to be of service, she avers, "I am happy to be a supply preacher every month or so. It gives me a chance to study and share my experiences without the burden of having to come with a message each week. I learn something new every time I preach and I want to keep on learning." She notes happily that she can be the recipient as well as the giver of grace. "I now have a pastor to count on, someone I can call on when life is out of control and I feel weak." Sharon trusts the traditions of the church as well as her decades in ministry to be both the launching pad for new adventures and a stable reality as she faces the challenges of aging.

Gordon Forbes, who was pastor of the church I attended during my years as Protestant University Chaplain and Professor of Theology at Georgetown University, noted that if he did not do something novel on the Monday following his retirement celebration, his car would automatically take him back to church.[5] He chose to head in the opposite direction, driving to Harper's Ferry, West Virginia, where he sat on a rock by the Potomac River and wrote a poem in which he describes his newfound status:

I watch thirty ninth graders board the shuttle-
    field trip to the National Park.
They'll learn of Union and Confederate maneuvers,
    hear of cannon, rifles, insurrection.
I will ignore this history today.
I feel pulled toward the river
    to a rock at the spot
where the legs of two rivers meet.
The wind peels leaves,
    just past peak, twirls them
    to rushing currents. River
receives their fluttering, carries them
downstream. Rocks and whirlpools
ahead, the tumble over Great Falls,
headed for the bay. Conception,
    birth, death converge.
The white spire of St. Peter's church
    juts like a needle above the trees,
points to heaven. But I have not come
for heaven. I come to watch leaves

just past peak, get carried away to
places they cannot imagine
on this first day of my retirement.[6]

Each moment emerges from the past and leans toward the future. Each present moment is a creative synthesis, a unique artistic creation, bringing together gifts and challenges of the past and yearning for a hopeful future. When pastors retire or begin to consider retirement, their lives are not a clean slate but a living document of experiences, skills, and insights. They have lifetime of successes and failures, gifts and talents, relationships and dreams, upon which to draw as they look toward the future. The concreteness of the past provides limits and boundaries. It also is the womb of possibility and creativity.

After retiring from full-time pastoral ministry, Gordon Forbes became an active member of a suburban Maryland congregation and served as the chair of the board of a large suburban church. He continues to write poetry and mentor younger pastors, using his experience as a source of guidance and wisdom for the next generation of congregational leaders. He has also regularly taught poetry to inmates at the Montgomery County Jail. His understanding of God as calling us toward the future and challenging the status quo motivated his own quest for novelty and creativity in retirement.

Paul, a Western Pennsylvania United Church of Christ pastor, finds joy in being chairperson of his congregation's worship committee. "I can use my liturgical gifts to support the mission of the church without being the final word in worship." A gifted communicator and writer, Paul spends a good deal of his retirement giving talks at retirement homes related to finding meaning in life. He continues to write regularly, building on the foundation of forty years of composing weekly sermons. "Writing comes easily and when do my daily writing, even if it's only a few paragraphs, I feel like I'm living out my calling and making a contribution to the spiritual lives who will read my words."

As Hammarskjold says, "for all that has been—thanks!" Claiming your life, perhaps through a life review or journey to congregations where you have served can energize the spirit for the "yes" that shall be. In the Spring of my sixty-sixth year, 2019, I took a week to travel around Northern California, going to the places I'd lived and reclaiming fifty-year friendships. In many ways, I lived out T. S. Eliot's affirmation: "*We* shall not cease from exploration, and the end of all our exploring will be to arrive where *we* started and know the place for the first time." Particularly poignant was preaching at Grace Baptist Church, the church of my college years, where I first experienced the call to ministry. In the course of my sermon, I gave thanks for my

mentors, John Akers and George L. "Shorty" Collins, the pastors who saw
a scholar-minister in a long-haired hippie kid, and recalled some of the lay
"saints" of the church who modeled the meaning of faithful ministry. Forty-
five years, in 2019, after I preached my first sermon at Grace, I was once again
in the pulpit, preaching on the week after Easter, reflecting on the faithfulness
of Thomas, whose doubt was a catalyst to sharing the good news in India. The
church was celebrating 100 years of ministry, and I was moved when I saw
a photograph of myself from 1974, a college junior delivering groceries to a
shut-in. "Hey, that long-haired kid is me!" I mused as I gave thanks for a past
that inspired and undergirded my ministry nearly five decades ago.

Relationship Is Everything

Desmond Tutu popularized the word "ubuntu" to describe the interdependence of life. As Tutu uses this Southern African word, it means "I am
because we (or you) are." We are, as Martin Luther King, Jr. affirmed inex-
tricably related to one another in the interdependent fabric of life. Our joys
and sorrows are one. Or, as the Apostle Paul put it, "If one member suffers,
all suffer together with it; if one member is honored, all rejoice together with
it" (I Corinthians 12:26). God comes to us in our relationships and these relationships open us to new possibilities for self-discovery and ethical action.

Pastors are, by definition, relational people, whether they are by disposition introverts or extroverts. In my Cape Cod village church context, I
professionally encounter well over a hundred people each week, sometimes
with a brief word, other times for counsel, adult education, or conversation
about a congregational or village issue. Although I have strong professional
boundaries, some of these people have become dear friends. Their well-being
matters to me. When a congregant I have gotten to know well dies or begins
to falter physically or intellectually, I grieve. More than once, I have become
verklempt in the course of a memorial service for a beloved congregant. I
have good friends across the country, and some relationships spanning over
fifty years. Still, my primary day-to-day relationships here on Cape Cod are
with my congregants and my family. This can be source of great joy as well
as grief and loneliness when a pastor leaves their congregation. It may even
be more difficult for clergy spouses for whom the congregational groups are
often their primary relational community.

Sharon describes her great sense of loss, when she retired from a congregation where she served for fourteen years. "I really missed that community.
I know I needed to preserve good boundaries so that church could transfer
its pastoral allegiance to my successor. Still, it was difficult." Diane, a
Connecticut Episcopalian pastor with whom I met, found herself in conflict
with her successor when she continued to get together for movies or dinners

with a handful of former congregants. "It was tough to let go and it was more difficult for my husband who had led the men's group for several years," she confessed, "but finally we did. I still miss them." Sharon's husband found it especially difficult, as he noted in our conversation, and wanted to stay in the congregation after she left. Eventually, he realized that this would create problems for Sharon. After a few years away from the congregation, he has resumed playing golf with some of his friends from church, enjoying the camaraderie, but staying out of congregational conversations.

In an interdependent, relational, and open-ended universe, pastors need to affirm the importance of relationships as a source of creativity, new ideas, intimacy, and mutual support. They need to grieve the loss of pastoral relationships while also discovering appropriate boundaries for relationships with former congregants, knowing that "one size does not fit all" pastoral relationships or boundary setting. Retirement creates new possibilities for marriage and family and opens the door for new gifts and graces.

Tom and Susan, a United Church of Christ clergy couple, both ordained for over forty years, enjoy travel and leisurely afternoons together. While they are still struggling to make new friends outside of the church and professional relationships, they rejoice in the opportunity to spend time with their grandchildren. Tom admits, "When we were in the parish, we had to work around our church schedules to make time for our children and later our grandchildren. Now, we see our children and grandchildren a few times a week. We volunteer at grandchildren's schools and have them for a sleep over at least once a week."

Although Susan experienced grief over leaving her relationships at church, her daily time activities of picking up her young grandchildren, working on justice-related issues, and taking classes at the senior center, more than compensates for their loss. "It truly takes a village to raise a family these days. My husband and I spend our afternoons supervising homework, and going to movies, dance lessons and little league with the grands. We provide time and treats and our grandchildren and our own lives are enriched. This is truly the best life."

Other pastors embody the relational nature of life in the realm of politics and social change. The theological perspectives that guided their ministries still guide them and now they do not have to worry about ruffling congregational feathers. Sally made a commitment when she retired in 2017 to devote much of her discretionary time to the combating global climate change, which she sees as a matter of life and death for her grandchildren, their children, and the nonhuman world. "When we elected a climate denier as president, that was the last straw. I knew I had to do something. I didn't want my grandchildren to ask me, 'Where were you when the glaciers melted and the seas rose?'" Sally goes to environmental meetings, advocates for clean energy, writes letters to her representatives, and marches for climate justice, where she still wears her collar and has been arrested twice. "It's all connected," she asserts, "justice toward women, immigrants, the LGBTQ+ community, and the environment. The same people who deny climate also deny equal rights and separate children from their parents. Now, that I don't have to deal with church politics or please the more conservative members of my congregation, I can deal with real politics. I can be prophet and protester, without counting the cost to my congregation and myself."

In a world of intricate interdependence, our relationships can transform our grandchildren and the planet. We can truly claim our responsibility to be partners with God in confronting injustice and healing the earth.

God Is in This Place, and Now I Know It

One night, the patriarch Jacob retreated to a solitary spot. In the course of the night, he dreamed of a ladder of angels, going from earth to heaven and then back down to earth. He awakened with amazement and awe and stammered, "Surely the LORD is in this place—and I did not know it! . . . How awesome is this place! This is none other than the house of God, and this is the gate of heaven" (Genesis 28:16–17). Rabbi Abraham Joshua Heschel asserted that radical amazement is at the heart of the spiritual adventure. Truly, Jacob was amazed and overwhelmed and called the place of his vision, "Beth-El," the gateway to heaven.

If God is omnipresent, then God is with us, seeking wholeness and providing guidance in every situation and encounter. "The whole earth is full of God's glory," Isaiah discovers in the Temple (Isaiah 6:1–8, AP). John's Gospel proclaims that the "true light which enlightens everyone was coming into the world" (John 1:9) and the Gnostic Gospel of Thomas proclaims, "Cleave the wood and I [the Christ] am there" (77). Every moment is a potential epiphany in which the doors of perception, as William Blake asserts, may be cleansed and we can see reality as it is in all its infinity.

The journey of retirement is filled with adventure. We can try on new identities, learn new words to describe ourselves, and face the necessary losses as well as joys that accompany the aging process. Still, God is with us and every moment can be revelatory for those who awaken to the Living God.

On the journey of retirement, pastors need to become attentive to what Jean-Pierre de Caussade (1675–1751) described as the "sacrament of the present moment." According to the French mystic, God still speaks today as he spoke to our forefathers in days gone by."[7] Those who open their eyes to holiness discover, as the joke goes, that "God is like Elvis, you'll see him everywhere!" In describing Jacob's encounter with God to a nun he was counseling, de Caussade asserted:

> You are seeking God, dear sister, and he is everywhere. Everything proclaims him to you, everything reveals him to you, everything brings him to you. He is by your side, over you, around and in you. Here is his dwelling and yet you still seek him . . . You seek perfection and it lies in everything that happens to you—your suffering, your action, your impulses, are the mysteries under which God reveals himself to you.[8]

We are standing on Holy Ground, and whether we are in the heights or depths, God is our companion. This is at the heart of Dan's experiential theology, inspiring him constantly to ask, "Where is God in all of this?" and "What is the work God is calling me to do?" It also motivates Susan's environmental advocacy and recognition of the importance of preserving endangered species and ensuring a livable planet for future generations.

We practice for retirement by recognizing and transforming the theological affirmations that guided us throughout our ministry. Yet, the letting go, characteristic of retirement from full-time ministry, creates space to focus more explicitly on God's presence in our lives. For many pastors, this becomes a Christian equivalent of the final stages of the spiritual journey, enshrined in Hindu spirituality, in which our primary task is to become attentive to God's presence in the present moment and in our quest to become fully alive in companionship with our Creator. The mystic quest has become central to Stephen's retirement. This Lutheran pastor notes, "Now that I am retired, I have time to pray, meditate and go on retreats. Prayer was always part of my ministry. But, often, I was too rushed to go deep. Now, I spend my days in study and meditation. Freed from the busyness of ministry, I take time to pause and notice God in my interactions throughout the day."

Companionship with God in Changing the World

In his final counsel to his followers, Jesus reminded them, "Lo, I am with you always, to the end of the age" (Matthew 28:20). Like those who walked with Jesus on the path to Emmaus, we can discover that God is with us on the way, wherever that road takes us. God not only guides and protects us, but also inspires us to action. The departing Jesus left his followers with a task, to "go into all the world, and preach the good news to all creation" (Mark 16:15). This is still our calling and the world we confront with good news is the complicated, intricately connected, complex, and fragile planet in all its wondrous diversity. Jesus knew that the future of God's realm "on earth as it is in heaven" requires a divine–human synergy. The future is open-ended, and our efforts may make the difference between life and death for ourselves, the vulnerable, and our planet. In that spirit, Pamela's recognition that small actions can make a great difference has been a motivating factor in her volunteering as a concierge at a clinic and social service center for the vulnerable and homeless community. This retired Disciples of Christ pastor affirms that "she is doing ministry by treating the visitors with respect and bringing peace to the chaos of their lives." Like other retired pastors, who continue their ministries at soup kitchens, hospitals, nursing homes, and public schools, Pamela seeks to see Christ in everyone she meets and by her caring bring Christ forth in all Christ's hidden places.

Philosopher Alfred North Whitehead asserts that peace comes when we move from self-interest to world loyalty and identify our well-being with the well-being of our communities and the planet. This sense of world loyalty is central to Susan's involvement in the environmental movement. "I may never see the fruits of my work. But I am committed to bringing beauty to the lives of children I will never meet. I may not accomplish much on my own, but when I gather with others, we can do something great to save our planet. As I agitate and advocate for the environment, I feel that I am doing God's work as fully as I was in the pastorate. I am a pastor without portfolio, but my mission, to paraphrase John Wesley, is to the whole world."

The future is wide open and depends on our efforts as well as in God's. God needs our partnership to heal the earth. Without God's inspiration, we lack direction; but without our companionship and efforts, God will not achieve God's vision of Shalom, a healed and transformed world.

PATHWAYS TO JUBILEE

In my work with seminarians and new pastors, I counsel them to explore their deepest, non-negotiable theological beliefs. Your theological vision serves as guidepost for facing the challenges of ministry. It provides a broader perspective, a global story, within which the challenges and necessary losses of life can be understood and confronted. In the words of New Testament scholar and process theologian Will Beardslee, our theological vision provides a "house for hope"—a rock upon which we can stand—when our world is in upheaval. We can see the power of interdependent theological and spiritual visions in the affirmations of Psalm 46:

God is our refuge and strength,
    a very present help in trouble.
Therefore we will not fear, though the earth should change,
    though the mountains shake in the heart of the sea;
though its waters roar and foam,
    though the mountains tremble with its tumult . . .
Be still, and know that I am God!

I am exalted among the nations,
    I am exalted in the earth.
The LORD of hosts is with us;
    the God of Jacob is our refuge.

Exploring Theology for a New Season

In this spiritual–theological practice, I invite you to set aside an afternoon for reflection. You might choose to take a mini retreat at a park, library, cabin, or place where you can devote your full attention. In the solitude, consider the following questions, based on Psalm 46: What are my fundamental theological beliefs about God, human life, vocation, and the planet? In what ways do these beliefs shape my behavior and social involvement? In what ways do these beliefs serve as guideposts for my preparation for retirement or then during retirement? How can I more fully live out these beliefs?

Affirmations for the Journey

Create a series of affirmations, based on your current theological beliefs. These affirmations become a mini theology that can repeat regularly and prayerfully to provide guideposts for charting the journey ahead. Some of my theological affirmations include:

God is with me in every situation.
God constantly inspires me with creative and life-transforming ideas.
Wherever I am and in whatever situation in I find myself, God is with me.
Nothing can separate me from the love of God.
My vocation is to be God's companion in healing the world.
God is with me in every change.

As I look toward retirement and the realities of aging, I have composed a set of faithful affirmations:

God will guide me to new possibilities for service in my retirement.
Regardless of my physical condition, my spirit soars.
My creativity and wisdom are growing with each new day.
I use my free time faithfully and creatively.
I have all the time, talent, and treasure to personally flourish and serve others.

What affirmations shape your journey? Try repeating one or more of these throughout the day and invoking them in times of uncertainty and anxiety.

A Prayer for the Pathway. Loving and Creative Adventure, I give thanks for your presence in my life. I am grateful for your inspiration in the past and your presence in the future. Guide my steps as on the pathways to the future. Awaken me to your presence in persons and situations I encounter. In Christ's name. Amen.

NOTES

1. Real name.

2. H. Richard Niebuhr, *The Responsible Self: An Essay in Christian Moral Philosophy* (New York: Harper & Row, 1963), 126.

3. Real name, not pseudonym.

4. "Necessary losses" and "unfixables of life" are terms coined by Judith Viorst and Alan Jones, respectively.

5. Real name.

6. Gordon Forbes, *Downstream* (Bethesda, MD: Authorhouse, 2007). Quoted originally in Bruce Epperly and Katherine Epperly, *The Four Seasons of Ministry: Gathering a Harvest of Righteousness* (Herndon, VA: Alban Institute, 2008), 139–40.

7. Jean-Pierre de Caussade, *The Sacrament of the Present Moment* (New York: Harper San Francisco, 1982), 1.

8. Ibid., 18.

Chapter 3

Embarking on a Vision Quest

Now the LORD said to Abram [and Sarai], "Go from your country and your kindred and your father's house to the land that I will show you" . . . And Abram [and Sarai] journeyed on by stages toward the Negeb. (Genesis 12:1, 9, AP)

Indigenous North American youth often embarked on vision quests as they prepared for adulthood. Like Jesus' retreat in the wilderness, the aim of their vision quests was to face the challenges and temptations inherent in claiming one's vocation. These youth discovered that with great power comes great danger to our souls and to the souls of those we serve. They "cried for a vision," and for wisdom in charting their adult journeys.

As clergy, we too "cry for a vision," a path forward as we prepare for retirement and live out our retirement years. We know that with great adventure comes danger—the danger of becoming lost, rootless, and without direction; the danger of boredom and obsolescence, of rusting out rather than going forth. Pilgrims must calibrate their spiritual GPS to find their way through the unchartered territories of retirement.

When clergy retire from full-time, active ministry, this transition invites them to embark on a mature version of the vision quest. They must, as Joseph Campbell asserts, begin their own heroic journey with tests as well as triumphs lying ahead of them. Just as many of these clergy did fifty years earlier as youth or later in life, when they felt the first calls to ministry, retiring clergy recognize that transitions raise questions, surface insecurities, and challenge us to embrace new identities and vocations. We may in the spirit of the biblical tradition receive a new name, appropriate to our discovery of new gifts and callings. Midlife pastors remember these same stirrings, often unexpectedly occurring when they thought they had their personal and professional futures planned out!

For most pastors, the call of the future, embodied in retirement, requires a time of personal, spiritual, professional, and congregational preparation in which both pastor and congregants alike embrace new relationships and identities. As I stated earlier, such transitions are part of a heroic journey in which we must travel to unfamiliar places, face internal and external threats, and be initiated into new possibilities for using our gifts to serve the world. Although initially we may feel rootless and disoriented, we need to recall the wisdom of J. R. R. Tolkien's observation, "Not all those who wander are lost." Like Abraham, Sarah, and Saul of Tarsus, the crisis of unfamiliarity may lead to the discovery of new vistas and the joy of a new name.

This book emerged out of my own personal and professional vision quest. Now a member of the Medicare generation, after forty years of joining pulpit and study, hospital visitation, budget meetings, strategic congregational planning, preaching and teaching, I am on the verge of a new adventure. Within the next few years, I will move from full-time ministry to the borderlands of retirement from congregational and academic ministry. I will need to redefine my priorities, identity, and schedule. With an open future ahead of me, I will have to chart the landscape and make preparations, including adequate spiritual and relational provisions, if I intend for the journey to be a holy adventure, bringing me closer to God, my neighbor, and my calling for this season of life.

Over the past year, I have been fortunate to practice for retirement due to the grace of my "final" professional sabbatical. While my sabbatical had a clear focus, researching the dynamics of clergy retirement and involved interviews, research, and writing as well as rest and reflection, I also experienced the contours of what lies ahead: Sundays without sermons or even going to church; looking for the church I might choose to attend in retirement; days without required meetings, classes, or appointments. For the first time in four decades, for over a month, I was aware of hospitalizations, deaths, and memorial services of congregants that did not necessitate my pastoral care or liturgical leadership. In talking with dozens of retired pastors, I contemplated both the joys and pitfalls they experienced in preparing for their retirements and meditated on a future untethered from congregational leadership, board meetings, sermon writing, pastoral care, and worship leadership. I pondered what it would be like to continue living in our Cape Cod village home, just a mile from my current congregation, and observe appropriate boundaries, knowing that I would run into congregants on walks and at concerts, shopping trips, and the library adjacent to the church building. I also considered what it would be like to leave my beloved Cape to relocate in Washington DC if our son and daughter-in-law decided to relocate for business purposes. In either case, I would have to let go of my current way of life to fully embrace a new and creative adventure.

In the course of my sabbatical, I embarked on a "sentimental journey," returning to the Salinas Valley of my childhood, the San Jose foothills of my teen years, the college campus of my undergraduate years, and the idyllic town of Claremont, where I attended seminary, graduate school, and met my wife. I returned to my college church where I preached my first sermon in 1972 and had my first experiences as a teacher and worship leader. I renewed relationships with friends from fifty years back, all the while taking stock of my current relationships and my future needs for friends and professional activity. In my life review of successes, failures, achievements, and losses, I garnered unexpected resources for the adventure ahead. I had survived success and failure, conflict and calm, and would need to marshal my spiritual, intellectual, imaginative, physical, and relational resources for the next set of challenges.

In the wake of encounters with retired pastors, describing their own preparation for and first years of retirement, I discovered that I needed to intentionally erect guideposts for the journey. Prior to my professional departure from active ministry at South Congregational Church, United Church of Christ, I will need to revise my life map to orient me for the unexpected and expected changes retirement and aging bring. I will also begin to imagine how I would join structure and spontaneity in my daily life. I will have to imaginatively visualize where I, an introvert by disposition, would meet new friends as well as revive relationships I had placed on the back burner to attend to my professional life. Although my two grandsons are at the heart of my current life, I pondered their growing up as well as my own aging and recognized that within a decade they would be charting their own adventures in college and then marriage and family life just as I had done decades earlier, likely far from we are currently living. While they will always be in my heart, they will no longer be in my daily routines of transportation, homework, play, and personal counsel.

Moreover, after over forty years of joining professional responsibilities with marriage, I will also have to establish new patterns of positive activities with my wife in our more spacious daily and weekly schedules. Taking the first steps of preparation was both daunting and exciting, motivated by the question,

Who will I be when I am no longer pastor, professor, or spiritual leader? How will I describe myself as I meet new people? In what communities will I find spiritual nourishment? Where will I do during the day when I no longer have a study at a church or seminary? What will be my new haunts to meet folks and to get out of the house? Where will I be called to serve, and in what ways will I share my time and talents for the well-being of others?

I know that sometime in the future I will embark on a vision quest, a *wanderjahre*, in which I will be choosing new possibilities and a new way of life.

In the spirit of Viktor Frankl, the events of my retirement will be questioning me and presenting me with challenges for the journey ahead. Will it be a wilderness or a promised land, or a combination of both?

The fact that someday I would be leaving a vocation around which had defined my life for over forty years raised other questions. I felt like the Dante as he entered a place of chaos and possibility: "In the middle of the journey of our life I found myself in a dark wood where the straight road had been lost sight of." My retirement ruminations have led to thoughts of aging and physical diminishment, fears of dementia and Alzheimer's and living my final years in a nursing home, challenges to my sense of personal meaning, larger concerns related to the foolishness of world leaders and the world we are leaving to our grandchildren, and the ultimate realities of dying, death, and the beyond.

I realized with the Serenity Prayer that many events out of my control will inexorably occur, despite any efforts on my part to prolong the aging process or protect those whom I love. I will experience what Judith Viorst calls the "necessary losses" of aging, grief, changes in health, and death. I also recognized that how I will face life's necessary losses was partly in my hands and that in the words of philosopher Alfred North Whitehead, I had the freedom to create a life of "tragic beauty," a jubilee of gratitude as I faced my own mortality. I needed be intentional, yet open to novelty and surprise, as I made my preparations for the journey. Many things, after all, are in our power and in the jubilee years of aging and retirement, we can expand our visions inspired by new horizons of service, intellectual growth, relationships, and service. We can become Mahatmas, Bodhisattvas, and Little Christs!

Those who do not take agency in shaping their lives will soon lose what agency they have. As I create the contours of my retirement adventures, I need to listen to those who have sojourned ahead of me to find guideposts for my own jubilee years. Their retirement maps would provide guidance for my own map-making and for my first steps to a new and adventurous life.

THE CALL TO RETIREMENT

Tom, an actively retired Disciples of Christ minister, felt the first call to retirement through an unexpected life review. As he played with his grandchildren during a holiday at the beach, he recalled that his own children had never met their grandparents. Both died before they were seventy, and now he was pushing seventy himself. He loved his work and was so immersed in congregational and denominational work that he was on the go six or seven days each week, clocking in between sixty and seventy hours and never taking his allotted vacation and study time.

"I knew I needed to make a change. I loved the ministry. But I needed to spend more time with my wife and family. I wanted to see my grandchildren make it through the milestones of high school and college and maybe even marriage and family."

Tom began to work fewer hours at church, passing on certain responsibilities to the congregation's associate pastor. Recognizing that he needed to explore new ways of life, he began saying "no" to invitations to assume greater denominational responsibilities. Now two years into retirement at age sixty-nine, Tom is still involved in the church. He serves on the board of a ministry with refugees, goes to borderlands a week yearly to ensure the well-being of undocumented immigrants, and supply preaches once or twice a month. Tom admits that it was difficult to say goodbye to his congregation after twenty years as senior pastor. A lot of tears were shed during his six-month ramping down to retirement. But both church and Tom are doing well. The church called a competent interim minister who is inviting the congregation to imagine new visions of the future in tandem with creative and committed leadership. Tom admits, "I didn't think I would make it at first. You can't plan on the grief you experience. But now I love Sunday mornings when I can arrive at church at 10:55 a.m. and leave right after the service if I feel like it. I don't miss the yearly budget process and managing the deferred maintenance of a large facility. I feel blessed to take weekends away with my children and grandchildren. I've found a church where I feel at home, can enjoy Sundays holding hands with my wife in church, and helping out when I'm asked."

Bill, a West Coast United Methodist pastor, experienced what theologian Paul Tillich described as a "Kairos" moment. "It was the right time. I was healthy. The church was healthy. I still enjoyed preaching and pastoral care. I wanted to do something new. I come from a family known for its longevity and I wanted, God willing, to spend the next twenty-five years exploring my other gifts."

Bill took classes and workshops offered by the denomination's pension fund, read books on retirement, and spoke with other retired pastors. He and his wife met with their financial adviser and spoke with people from the pension office and decided that sixty-eight was the right time for retirement. Bill began to alert his congregation about his retirement a few years in advance. He did not have a set agenda or time frame but reminded them at age sixty-five that he did not expect to be in the pulpit until he was seventy. He met regularly with the congregation's pastoral relations committee to share what he was planning. When he finally retired after ten years of at the congregation, the church celebrated his ministry and named the new fellowship hall, a central component of the capital campaign he facilitated, after him.

Pam, a United Christ pastor now retired in Florida, had another type of "Kairos" moment. After a three-decade pastorate in an east coast suburb, she discerned that the community and church culture were changing faster than she could keep up with. Committed to excellence in worship, preaching, faith formation, and pastoral care, she no longer felt that she could respond to the corporate approach of the congregation's emerging leadership. She had completed successful capital campaigns, handled finances responsibly, and ensured the beauty and safety of the building. But, as she shared, "I no longer wanted to spend my time worrying about the bottom line, arguing about expenses, and managing staff challenges." Further, she admits, "I felt I was not the best person to address the challenges of the changing culture of Sunday sports, overcommitted families, and suburban professional life. It was somewhat jarring to realize that I had become old school while the church was living into new school. The church needed someone more agile and attuned to these changes. I was growing weary adjusting to the changing church culture."

Pam also began preliminary conversations with the church's leadership and denominational officials, exploring how best the church and she could ensure a positive and life-giving transition. "To my surprise," Pam admits, "there had already been conversations among the church's leaders. While they didn't want me to leave, they also knew I would eventually retire and wanted to honor me as well as prepare for the future."

Pam and her attorney-wife had purchased a vacation home in Florida several years before their retirement and this became their oasis and mecca and now their permanent residence. Pam believes that her timing of retirement enabled her to be grateful for three decades of ministry and hopeful for an active retirement, including occasional supply preaching, involvement in conference mentoring programs for new pastors and seminarians, and volunteering with Meals on Wheels as well as reading and painting. "I retired at just the right time for the church and myself. The church has found the right successor and is flourishing, and I am healthy and active in creating a new life here in Florida."

Carol also had a unique moment of decision. "I retired the day I closed the church." After working tirelessly for ten years first to grow the church and then to keep it alive, Carol and the leadership came to the realization that the congregation could no longer continue its visible ministry. "It was a jolt," she admits. "I had done everything I could. I tried program after program, but the demographics of the congregation were against us. With each death, the church's finances become more precarious until they reached the point that they could no longer pay the pastor." Carol describes her grief as twofold: "First, I grieved my new professional status. Who am I, now that I am no longer a pastor? Ordination is for life and yet I'm now an outsider among my former peers and congregants. I also grieved the loss of the congregation, and under my watch. I never imagined that I would be the one to close this church."

She confesses that for the first year she was "in the wilderness. I didn't go to church. I felt awkward at clergy groups." Now in her late sixties, Carol and her husband have joined a church near their home, and she is slowly becoming involved in the planning and participating in the worship service at the request of the congregation's pastor and leadership. Carol states that my prayer these days is "God show me what's to come next?"

Susan also felt that the time was right to retire. In her ten years of leading a mid-western United Methodist congregation, she had turned the church around: growing it from an average of twenty-five on Sundays to over two hundred and from a deficit to balanced budget. "I had exceeded my expectations. Our congregation voted to be reconciling with the LGBTQ community, refurbished the building, expanded its outreach to the homeless of our community, and adopted a five-year strategic plan. It was the right time for me to do something new. I wanted to travel with my husband, spend time with our grandchildren, and explore becoming a spiritual director."

After a six-month hiatus, Susan embarked on a two-year program with the Shalem Institute, based in Washington DC, and now regularly meets with five to ten spiritual directees each week. "I am doing what I always wanted to do in ministry—care for peoples' souls. I am energized, happy, and have more energy now than I did when I retired five years ago. Each day I feel blessed to wake up and serve God."

Janet, a suburban Northern California Baptist pastor, saw her sense of fatigue as a call to let of full-time ministry. "I had been a pastor for thirty years, preached over a thousand sermons, gone to hundreds of board meetings, and the thrill was gone. I was still operating at full-throttle and doing good work. But I was losing my passion. I no longer looked forward to sermon preparation, which was once the highpoint of my ministry. I was losing my passion for worship planning, another of my gifts. I needed a Sabbath. Not just a day, but maybe for the rest of my life!"

A year before she formally retired, Janet began to signal to her pastoral relations team that "I had about a year or so left in me. I was sixty-four and they understood. We prepared for my transitioning out." Three years after her retirement, Janet enjoys reading, golf, gardening, and travel. She has also accepted a position on her association's ministerial support committee. "I love mentoring seminarians and helping them learn healthy skills for ministry."

During my own sentimental journey through Northern California, I met Liliana, the senior pastor of the congregation who nurtured my call to ministry during college.[1] Grace Baptist was flourishing, a multicultural community open to the LGBTQ community as well as to persons with intellectual, emotional, and substance use challenges living in "board and care" homes. Six months later, I reached out to Liliana after I read on Facebook that she was planning to retire after Christmas. "Grace is an amazing church. But it was time for me to retire. I had some health issues and the stress and responsibilities of handling an urban church were wearing me down. I had put the church first and committed to staying until the church was in good shape. Our finances were in good shape and we had a strategic plan. Now it was time to pass the leadership to a younger person."

Although she had not chosen a date when we met earlier in the year, she was beginning to do her due diligence regarding congregational strategic visioning and ensuring the success of leasing the church's parking lot, a premium housing location, for the construction of a seven-story, hundred-unit apartment building that would secure the church's financial future.

In her early sixties, Liliana had run the race and run it well. She and her husband were happy to have lived near their sons for eight years. "Now it is time to live near our two daughters and six grandchildren in Portland, Oregon. We wanted to reduce our costs and recognized that our mortgage payment in Portland would be half of what we are paying in Silicon Valley. Ministry is a lifetime profession and though I won't be taking on a fulltime appointment, I will be open to preaching and consulting."

She was also recently elected chair of the Executive Committee of the Evergreen Baptist association, a progressive West Coast association in the American Baptist Churches.

In her resignation letter, Liliana shared her personal journey and hopes for the congregation:

> Grace Baptist Church has been the best church I had the privilege to minister during my whole experience in parish work. GBC is a relevant, vibrant, and authentic small Christian church where everyone is welcomed and embraced. In this corner of downtown, we have a great reputation based on our hands-on commitment to the plight of the poor, the mentally challenged, the suffering, and those who have experienced church rejection. People at GBC know how to love, and love for real.
>
> All of that makes Grace a high profile, very demanding and intense operation. Having experienced some health issues in the last year and feeling the need to restore from the wonderfully stressing work at GBC, retiring seems like the best option for me. Of course, my beloved husband is retiring as well; together, we are looking forward to serving the Lord at a slower pace, without the responsibilities this position entails. . . . It is sad to part ways, but when the wind of the Spirit blows, we must obey it. This is not goodbye because we still have three months to enjoy each other's partnership. Let's celebrate what the Lord is doing. God bless you.

Leaving with a blessing is our goal in our final congregational ministries—a blessing for our congregations and a blessing for the journey we will soon undertake.

Preparing for the Journey

Ron, a United Church of Christ pastor, now retired in the Southwest after forty years in ministry reflects, "Plan all you want, but don't expect it to work out the way you expected. Don't rush into things. Pause, take a breath, chart a course, and then expect surprises on the way." Preparation for retirement can be a spiritual practice in which we take time to listen to the sighs too deep for words, calling us to new personal and professional horizons.

As I contemplate the story of Abraham and Sarah's departure from Haran, I suspect that their response to the call of God was gradual rather than immediate. In my imagination, I see this semiretired couple assessing their finances, disposing of unnecessary possessions, and consulting with other pilgrims. They had a road map to their promised land, but despite all their careful preparations, they had many unexpected adventures. They discovered in a phrase popularized by John Lennon, "life is what happens when you're busy making other plans."

Faithful clergy retirement requires a sense of vision, but flexibility about your specific agenda to embrace the planned and unplanned events along the way.

For Peter, a Southern California Presbyterian pastor, spiritual and domestic decluttering characterized his retirement preparation. After years of being "too busy to go on retreat or practice meditation," Peter began to a daily practice of Centering Prayer, taking twenty minutes every morning for quiet communion with God. He found a spiritual director with whom he met on a monthly basis. He also contracted with a local counselor to reflect on issues of grief, forgiveness, and future planning. Physical decluttering mirrored his commitment to spiritual simplicity. He began to give away books he had accumulated in three decades of congregational ministry and seminary teaching. As he began to clear out his study, Peter decided that he would "only take as many books as I could put in the trunk of the car. Recognizing that I wanted to continue research and writing, I decided that I would utilize the seminary and community public libraries instead of buying new books. If I wanted a book, I would order a digital copy. This not only saves space, but also money."

A year after retirement, Peter moved to a beach community whose property values necessitated downsizing. "I am glad I anticipated this move in advance. My commitment to simplicity made the move less stressful and saved thousands of dollars in moving and mortgage expenses."

Cynthia, a retired Canadian Anglican priest and denomination executive, went on a monastic retreat five years before retiring. Her spiritual guide focused their conversations on the journey of the magi home by another way. Cynthia notes, "Home is retirement and I need to learn how to take a different way. I need to learn what the different things might me for me. What new roads I need to travel. You can't narrow down in retirement—you need to open up. Many clergy see themselves as narrowing down, downsizing and disappearing after retirement. In contrast, I have learned to be more open. I don't say I can't do this any more or can't do it now. I say maybe I can do it."

Cynthia's spiritual preparation enabled her to use her administrative experience and connections to serve on several boards, including one focusing on human trafficking.

Another forward thinker, a second-career United Church of Canada pastor, Sharon asked herself, "What will we do the week after retirement?" She recognized that she "needed to have a positive vision for the immediate as well as long term future." In that spirit, two days after her retirement party, Sharon and her husband Gordon "flew to Palm Springs where she soaked in sun while doing a three-week preaching and pastoral care stint at a local congregation. I didn't have to work very hard and we got to soak in plenty of sun for free." Upon returning to Nova Scotia, they packed their bags once more for a month-long sojourn in the Czech Republic.

Liz is a planner. She looks toward the future and then charts an ideal pathway toward her desired destination. "I've always been this way," she notes. "I like to plan a few steps ahead, or in the case of retirement, a few years ahead. I consider what's in my control and what isn't and maximize my agency in preparing for the future." A second-career Episcopalian pastor, who sought ordination after two decades in higher education administration, Liz decided that she would take several important steps toward retirement while serving in her final ministerial assignment. Living in the vicarage, she knew that she needed to purchase a home. She wanted to be near her son and two grandchildren, so after a year of house hunting, she found the ideal home three hours away her congregation and two miles from her family. Slowly and deliberately, she began transferring her personal and relational center to her future community, a New England college town. She chose to take a few days each month, settling into her new residence. She got to know the town, joined a few clubs, found a church she would attend, acquired a library card, and even pursued a few volunteer opportunities. Observing her methodical approach to retirement, her son quipped, "You know the town better than we do." For Liz, having a clear plan reflected her personality and made all the difference in the world. Not wanting to age by herself, this independent woman also took steps through Internet relationship sites for mature adults to meet new friends, including her current husband.

In contrast, Carolyn, a single Disciples of Christ pastor, who retired at sixty-three after thirty-five years of ministry, confesses "I wish I'd planned better for retirement. When I left my church of fifteen years, feeling that I had accomplished a great deal and was ready to move on, I had no idea of the void I would experience without a clear plan or something to look forward to."

An active, extroverted person, Carolyn felt alone and adrift for the first several months before finding her bearings and claiming her new role as a church consultant, hospice volunteer, and grandparent. What helped her through the wilderness was the personal support of a handful of pastors who heard her pain and shared their own retirement challenges.

Most pastors find themselves somewhere between Liz and Carolyn as they plan for retirement. Samuel, a Pennsylvania Mennonite pastor, sought God's guidance when he reached sixty-five. "I was healthy, still loved the ministry, and felt like I still had room to grow." After a personal retreat, meetings with his spiritual director, and consultation with the congregation's leadership team, Samuel stayed in active ministry for another five years. At seventy, Samuel "felt that God was leading him to a new adventure, focusing on responding to refugee resettlement and immigrants on United States borderland." Reflecting on his newfound vocation, Samuel states, "Now, I see my task as simply loving these newcomers and finding ways to respond to their most basic needs." Samuel has also joined the political fray, challenging the cruelty and vindictiveness he sees in the current U.S. immigration policy. "I have the White House, Homeland Security, and our Congressional representatives on speed dial. Not a week goes by that I don't advocate for compassionate hospitality for immigrants, regardless of their nation of origin or status. I've even be arrested twice at peaceful demonstrations. To me, this is what it means to see Jesus in the least of these."

A dear friend of mine, Suzanne, eased her transition into retirement by having a vision for life beyond church leadership.[2] A voracious reader and planner, she pored over texts on clergy retirement, looking for best practices that she might embody in her own process. She also enrolled as a participant in author and spiritual guide Parker Palmer's "The Soul of Aging" program. Suzanne prayerfully pondered how she might be of service in her retirement and found that her own experience could be a resource for clergy and laypersons preparing retirement. Extroverted by nature, Suzanne intentionally expanded her circle of friends beyond the church and her professional colleagues. A positive thinker, Suzanne prefers the word "graduation" to retirement. Although she was intentional about her own preparation, Suzanne admits that "despite our preparations for retirement, the only way to go through it is *to go through it!*" And, let the clergy say "Amen!"

PATHWAYS TO JUBILEE

In his *Tuesdays with Morrie,* harried newspaper columnist Mitch Albom asks his dying college professor Morrie Schwartz to describe his perfect day. The wise professor responds with a litany of apparently ordinary events:

awakening to a simple breakfast, going for a swim, being with friends and family, going for a walk and rejoicing in the beauties of nature, a dinner of duck, dancing, and then a good night's sleep. Initially, Albom is dissatisfied at his professor's response:

> It was so simple. So average. I was actually a little disappointed. I figured he'd fly to Italy or have lunch with the President or romp on the seashore or try every exotic thing he could think of. After all these months, lying there, unable to move a hand or foot—how could he find perfection in such an average day. Then I realized this was the whole point.[3]

The Jesuit mystic Jean-Pierre de Caussade (1675–1751) speaks of the sacrament of the present moment, experiencing God's providence in ordinary and unnoticed events of life. Our planning for retirement and the retirement jubilee itself is lived out one moment at a time in the undramatic and only occasionally dramatic moments of our lives. We can prepare for the Jubilee Years, but our preparation is most fruitful if it is grounded in discovering our joy, giftedness, vocation, in the Holy Here and Now of each day and season of life.

In this Jubilee practice, which may take several days or even weeks and will shift as time goes by, imagine your "perfect day." As always, begin your spiritual practice, prayerfully asking for God's guidance in your contemplations and your openness to the congruence of God's vision and your own personal vision. How would you spend a day in your current life setting with your current ministerial commitments? What events and encounters would bring joy, meaning, and holiness to your life? Let your mind wander without any need to please anyone but yourself and God.

Now, look ahead to your own perfect day and then a perfect season of your retirement. Unencumbered by the daily tasks—administration, meetings, paperwork, perhaps even sermons, classes, and pastoral care—what would your perfect retirement day look like? Or given a variety of interests and new callings, what would a perfect week or month look like? Again, let your mind wander without any need to please anyone but yourself and God.

Now visualize a six-month span of your retirement. What would activities and commitments would characterize a perfect season of retirement?

Then, taking time for further reflection, consider what practices you need to embody today, in your current season of your life, as the foundations for faithful, meaningful, and joyful seasons of retirement. Prayerfully, make a commitment to—one day at a time—create your future visions of retirement by your fidelity to God's vision in the Holy Here and Now.

A Prayer for the Pathway. God of this holy moment and every moment to come, awaken me to the intersection of today's plans and tomorrow's possibilities. Help me to choose what is truly important in this sacramental moment. Grant me a sense of your long-term vision for my life, lived out one moment at time is unrepeatable day. In Christ's Name. Amen.

NOTES

1. Real name.
2. Her actual name.
3. Mitch Albom, *Tuesdays with Morrie* (New York: Doubleday, 1997), 176.

Chapter 4

The Body Is the Temple

Or do you not know that your body is a temple of the Holy Spirit within you, which you have from God, and that you are not your own? For you were bought with a price; therefore glorify God in your body. (I Corinthians 6:19–20)

With greater life spans and overall well-being among the privileged classes in North America, shibboleths such as "sixty is the new fifty," "seventy is the new fifty-five," and "if you've got your health, you've got everything" have become commonplace in the media and everyday conversations. North Americans are a health-obsessed people. We want not only to live well but also to look good. Senior adults are portrayed by the media as active, affluent, and agents of new adventures, despite the fact that many retirees have less than a thousand dollars in the bank and must choose between paying their heating bills and purchasing much-needed medications.

I must admit that I enjoy watching Hallmark movies and classic television programs from the 1950s and 1960s. Aimed at my generation and demographics, the commercials that pop up every ten minutes or so reflect the concerns of people of my age group—over sixty, relatively affluent, hoping to enjoy a good life in retirement, and able to pursue hobbies and travel. In the course of one recent Sunday afternoon, relaxing after church, I was also regaled by advertisements related to weight loss, diabetes, irritable bowel syndrome, bladder leakage, strokes, dental implants, hearing aids, and cancer. The actors were, for the most part happy and energetic embodiments of the adage, "better living through chemistry!" The only exceptions were commercials asserting the importance of home caregivers for our aging parents and grandparents who want to "age in place" and medications that can stem the inexorable deterioration brought about by memory loss. In these commercials, these once active elders, our mothers and fathers, were portrayed as fragile, befuddled, and dependent, and now in need the protection of the children they had raised. We may chuckle at the images of the phrase, "I've fallen and I can't get up," but if we live alone or our companions are away on holiday, we feel more vulnerable and are more careful about trips to the basement or upper levels of our homes as I do when my wife is out of town or away for an extended length of time.

One of my best laugh lines in conversations with friends is "I'm still in midlife, provided to live to be 134." With each new birthday, I must revise the figure by two years, and recognize the tension between being active and vital in my mid-to-late sixties, now, and the reality that it is unlikely that I will make to 130!

As I write these lines, now midway through my sixty-seventh year, I am grateful for what I believe to be good physical, emotional, relational, and spiritual health. I am active professionally, regularly travel across the country and overseas for holidays and speaking engagements, enjoy good food and physical mobility, and can do most of the things I did at thirty, albeit at slower pace. I wake up with minimal pain and start each day around 4:30 a.m. with contemplative prayer, strong coffee, study and writing, and a sunrise walk on one of the Cape Cod's beautiful beaches. I feel truly blessed. I retire most nights watching a program on nature or politics or one of my favorite British mysteries, happily weary and ready to awaken to the next day. I know I am blessed and give thanks, although I know everything can change in a New York minute! As I write these words, I know that this is especially evident as congregations, like my own, around the country are suspending worship services as a result of COVID-19, the Coronavirus!

Still, my body reminds me that I am no longer sixteen or thirty-six. Despite Deepak Chopra's promise of "ageless body, timeless mind" and my own overall well-being, I seldom feel timeless these days. Although I walk two to three miles each day, I have discovered that when I play soccer, basketball, baseball, or superheroes with my grandchildren, I can no longer sprint without becoming winded. To tell the truth, I can no longer sprint! I wear magnifying glasses—"cheaters"—to help me read and type, and even with magnification I can no longer read the small print on legal documents or the Rand McNally Road Atlas. Without noticing it, I have become overweight. I cannot claim to be the rail-thin, long-haired, 140-pound hippie of 1970, the year of my high-school graduation! Without any unique moral or spiritual virtue on my part, I have never been diagnosed with a chronic illness, cancer, or mobility issues. Yet, this year, I broke my first bone and experienced several weeks of dermatitis. I belong in the categories of "worried well" and "anxious affluent" as I look toward the future. Knowing that everything could change with a fall, stroke, heart attack, infectious disease or gradual memory loss frightens me.

SERENITY AND CHANGE IN THE AGING PROCESS

Despite Deepak Chopra's assurances, there is no such thing as an "ageless body," although we can, within limits, be agents of our own well-being and practice behaviors to continue experiencing physical health in our retirement years. As my clergy contemporaries and I search for creative responses to the aging process, we are invited to consider the wisdom of the Serenity Prayer:

God, grant me the serenity to accept the things I cannot change,
Courage to change the things I can,
And wisdom to know the difference.

We might also cultivate the fighting spirit portrayed by an alternative vision of the Serenity Prayer that I recently found on Facebook and attributed to the political activist Angela Davis, an icon of my youth:

I'm no longer accepting the things I cannot change.
I am challenging the things I cannot accept.

Certain aspects of the aging process are out of my control. If I am fortunate, I will live long enough to attend my grandchildren's college graduation and perhaps their weddings and the birth of their own children. I look forward to growing older and slowing my professional pace to enjoy travel and uninter-rupted time for study and writing, but with the years I will experience certain forms of diminishment that cannot entirely be prevented by lifestyle, exercise, diet, spiritual practices, or medication. I need to accept these to experience peace of mind. Still, I trust the wisdom of a variation on the Serenity Prayer, embodied in Angela Davis' response, addressed to our current political situ-ation and other untenable realities in our lives: "God grant me the courage to change the things I cannot accept!" and let me protest what I cannot accept by challenging myself to ongoing physical well-being, and work hard to go beyond self-imposed physical, intellectual, and spiritual limitations.

I know that I do not have to be a victim of the aging process. My life, and yours, involves an interplay of responding to brute facts of life, the impact of the environment and aging, by affirming our own personal agency. In each moment, we have the freedom to shape our own destiny out of the materials life gives us. Accordingly, many aspects of the aging process are in my control. I can make healthy choices regarding physical activity, diet, rest, relationships, and involvement in my community. I can watch my weight, take care of my dental hygiene, reduce unnecessary stress, and take prescribed medications. I can maintain positive relationships with my wife, involving shared values, common tasks, and ongoing affection. I can wisely recognize and accept my mortality and the limitations of the years. I can also embrace the concrete limitations of life as the womb of possibility and vocation, and the place where I am called to be faithful to God, my companions, and future generations. As the philosopher Alfred North Whitehead asserts, God's vision for any given moment, situation, or season of life is "the best for that impasse" and not always ideal, in this concrete moment, I can embrace the Holy Here and Now and say "yes" to the life I have and the possibilities before me! I can also push past perceived limitations to embody new possibilities!

BIBLICAL VISIONS OF HEALTH AND WHOLENESS

Embodiment is at the heart of biblical world view. The message of the Genesis creation stories is that the physical world of stars, seas, whales, chimpanzees, and humankind is inherently good, a reflection of divine love and wisdom. Chaos and mortality exist among creatures of the earth like us. Yet, within interplay of providence, freedom, and chaos, humans may become God's culture and religion-creating partners. Even after the tragedy of their fall from innocence, Adam and Eve are given the resources to begin again, create a family, and become the parents of civilization.

The biblical vision describes God as active in the historical process, providentially guiding our personal lives as well as the historical process, and God's wise guidance includes energizing our bodies as well as our spirits, and our cells as well as our souls. In the biblical tradition, issues of pregnancy and health are important to God as vehicles of revelation and transformation. Filled with radical amazement at humankind, body, mind, and spirit, the Psalmist proclaims:

For it was you who formed my inward parts;
  you knit me together in my mother's womb.
I praise you, for I am fearfully and wonderfully made.
  Wonderful are your works;
that I know very well. (Psalm 139:13–14)

The Psalmist is not giving us a lesson in anatomy or physiology. The Psalmist is sharing his sense of wonder and gratitude at life itself and the amazing and intricate complexity of his whole being, body, mind, and spirit. Our whole lives—body, mind, and spirit—are a gift from God and our responsibility is to glorify God in our own physical well-being as well as promoting the physical well-being of others through just and compassionate political and social structures.

Years ago, while studying at the Shalem Institute for Spiritual Formation in Washington DC, I learned a simple chant, "I think you God for the wonder of my being." We are, as children of divine creativity, formed in the image of God and "awesomely" made. Billions of years of evolution, intricately weaving together divine providence, chance, and freedom, have brought forth human life and our wondrous planet in all its glory. We are star stuff, as cosmologists proclaim; we are also "the temple of the Holy Spirit within you," as the Apostle Paul declares (I Corinthians 6:19). Our bodies are the sanctuaries that support our spiritual and ethical quests and reflect our fidelity to God in our professional lives and social commitments. We can truly thank God for "the wonder of our being!"

The faith we affirm is incarnational. Isaiah is transformed and guided to his vocation as a prophet of Divine Shalom as he hears the angelic chant, "The whole earth is full of God's glory" (Isaiah 6:3). The Psalmist is overwhelmed as he discovers that everything that breathes can praise God (Psalm 150:6). The Word, the Logos and Sophia of God, that "became flesh" in Christ is grounded in God's creative wisdom, giving life, beauty, and order to all creation, including the wholistic integration of body, mind, and spirit (John 1:1–3, 14). When the author of John 1 affirms that "the true light, which enlightens everyone, was coming into the world" (John 1:9), he is surely referring to our whole being: our cells, our soul, our immune system, and our intellect. In a God-inspired and created world, "the heavens are telling the glory of God" (Psalm 19:1) and our intestines, circulatory system, and immune and reproductive systems give witness to divine artistry. God loves our bodies with the same passion that God loves our souls. The wonder of our being, nested in this glorious universe, challenges us to take our role as companions of our creator with the vocation "glorify God in our body" (I Corinthians 6:20). As Paul counsels in I Corinthians (6:12–20), how we treat our bodies and the bodies of others reveals our relationship with God and one another. When we glorify God with our bodies, we rejoice in our personal embodiment, honoring our bodies with appropriate care and affirmation, and reaching out to honor the bodies of others through acts of respect and justice-seeking.

DO YOU WANT TO BE HEALED?

Jesus proclaimed that God wants us to have abundant life in body, mind, and spirit (John 10:10). When God's energy of love moves within our lives, God can "accomplish abundantly far more than we can ask or imagine" (Ephesians 3:20). Well-being is our legacy as God's beloved children.

In the course of our professional lives as pastors, we have proclaimed the love of God, nurturing and giving life to all creation. We have taught the importance of faith in personal transformation and as a factor in activating God's energy and power in our lives and communities. Our ministries have touched bodies and spirits. We have baptized babies and youth, anointed the sick, and laid hands on congregants as we prayed for their healing. We have counseled people on lifestyle issues and comforted the dying and grieving. We have been cheerleaders for healing and wholeness, inviting our congregants to do the hard work of personal transformation, recovery, and physical and spiritual well-being. Yet, one of the ironies of ministry is that we have not always followed our own counsel in terms of lifestyle, physical well-being, and relationships. Like the lover of Song of Songs, "they made me keeper of the vineyards, but my own vineyard I have not kept!" (Song of Songs 1:6). At times, we have been so concerned for caring for others that we have forgotten to access the resources for healing and wholeness in our own lives. That insight came to Tom, a retired congregational and conference minister, when a layperson asked, "Ministers don't ever retire. Isn't your ministerial vocation lifelong?" Tom recalls that "at that moment, I realized that although was no longer in fulltime ministry, I still had a vocation and now my vocation was to take care of my vocation, my ability to share God's good news, and to practice what I'd preach to other pastors, and to take care of myself."

Gwen Wagstrom Halaas, family physician, pastor's spouse, and leader in ministerial wellness programs, gives a sobering account of overall clergy well-being in her *Clergy, Retirement, and Wholeness: Looking Forward to the Third Age.*[1] While some of her statistics come from the first decade of the twenty-first century, they still broadly apply to clergy I know, seminarians I have taught, and a large percentage of retired pastors. A study of Lutheran clergy, with an average age of fifty, indicated that two out of three Lutheran pastors were overweight, one out of three was obese, and nearly one out of five suffered from serious depression in the past year.[2] Duke University's Clergy Health Initiative study, completed in 2014, found that among retired United Methodist ministers, living in North Carolina, nearly 80 percent of the men and 70 percent of the women were overweight.[3]

Looking at the demographics of aging, and clergy are no exception in terms of health challenges, among persons over sixty-five, both clergy and lay, the leading causes of death in order are heart disease, cancer, stroke, chronic respiratory illness, influenza and pneumonia, and Alzheimer's disease.[4] While we cannot prevent every health crisis, it is clear that certain behaviors—unhealthy diet, physical inactivity, abuse or overuse of alcohol, smoking—increase our risk of serious illness and diminish our quality of life in retirement.

Many pastors have cared for others' well-being but neglected their own self-care. Long-hours, multi-tasking, overcommitment and co-dependence, job-related stress, congregational conflict and expectations, as well as

consumption of fast foods and inadequate physical activity have characterized their ministerial lifestyles, and now they are paying the price. As they
reach retirement age, many pastors are discovering that years of neglecting
their bodies is taking its toll in terms of decreased overall well-being as
well as energy level along with the incidence chronic ailments and slower
recovery from illness. Although studies indicate that religious activity is a
positive factor in overall health and that "prayer is good medicine," many
pastoral caregivers' neglect of positive relationships, lifestyle habits, and
spiritual practices are factors in decreased physical, emotional, and spiritual
well-being.

Despite Jesus' holistic vision of spirituality and healing, many pastors see
the body as a hindrance rather than a help in ministry, something we must
deal with rather than celebrate. In speaking about our attitudes toward food
and drink in ways that apply to our attitudes toward embodiment in general,
theologian Stephanie Paulsell queries:

> Is food our friend or enemy? Is it a gift to be received with thankfulness or a
> problem to be mastered? It is not surprising that our questions about food are
> nearly identical to our questions about our bodies . . . How we understand our
> bodies—as friend or enemy, as gift or as problem, as sacred and as repulsive,
> as temple of God's spirit or as a shell in which we are trapped—will influence
> how and what we eat and drink.[5]

The words of the apostle Paul to the Christian community at Rome invite us
to wholistic spiritual transformation, which embraces our bodies as well as
our spirits and inspires to be agents of healing in our communities.

> I appeal to you therefore, brothers and sisters, by the mercies of God, to pres-
> ent your bodies as a living sacrifice, holy and acceptable to God, which is your
> spiritual worship. Do not be conformed to this world, but be transformed by the
> renewing of your minds, so that you may discern what is the will of God—what
> is good and acceptable and perfect. (Romans 12:1–2)

Our attitudes about embodiment and its connection with God's vision for our
lives shape our lifestyles. As Paul noted (I Corinthians 10:23–31), followers
of God are free to follow a variety of dietary practices and lifestyle choices;
however, our freedom calls us to follow activities that promote wholeness of
body, mind, spirit, and our faith community. The renewing of our minds takes
us beyond our culture's understanding of health and beauty toward what is
authentically healthy for each of us at our age and station in life. When we
are in sync with God's personal vision for our health and well-being, we will
have the energy we need for relationships, sports and hobbies, family life, and

service to the church, community, and the planet. There are no ideal physical norms as we age and those who live with limitations brought on by disease, disability, or aging process can still practice healthy lifestyles and serve God in their unique calling. No one is excluded from God's grace, vision of possibility, or contribution to healing the earth. Nor should illness be a catalyst for judgment or self-recrimination. When God's grace abounds, enlivening our cells and souls alike, we can begin again, choosing healthy life patterns that minimize the impact of past neglect.

Jesus once encountered a man whose illness had confined him to a healing site for thirty-eight years (John 5:2–18). When confronted with the question, "Do you want to be made well?" he initially did not reply in the affirmative. Instead, he gave a reason for his ongoing paralysis: no one would help him to the healing pool. Not content with his answer, Jesus commanded, "Stand up, take up your mat and walk." Trusting Jesus for his healing, in that moment of decision, the man stood up and walked. The dramatic healing is not the end of the story. It was the Sabbath and his healing caused a stir among the religious leaders. He was walking, carrying his mat, having forgotten such activity was prohibited by Sabbath law. Asked why he was carrying his mat, his response was curious, "The man who made me well said 'Take up your mat and walk.'" When Jesus encounters the man later in the day, Jesus' response seems harsh and appears to return to the rewards–punishments theology. Jesus challenges in his encounter with a sight-impaired man, recorded in John 9: "See, you have been made well! Do not sin anymore, so that nothing worse happens to you." I believe Jesus' response is aimed at the man's lifestyle and spiritual life and is not intended as a threat of divine punishment for his passivity. Now that he is healed, he must claim his well-being one moment at a time. He must actively move forward in his life, become an agent of destiny, not a passive victim of fate. His issue involved both physical and spiritual paralysis, and from now on he must be actively engaged in his own healing process.

Jesus' words are addressed to clergy at every season of ministry, including clergy considering retirement or already retired. "Do you want to be made well? Is health and well-being of vital interest to you? Do you want have the energy and vitality to claim your place as God's companion in healing the world or will you jeopardize your vocation by passively maintaining lifestyle habits that increase your risk of serious illness and debilitation?"

This is a question of spirituality and vocation. Our bodies, like our time, talent, and treasures, are vocational and are the instruments through which we faithfully serve God. As we look toward active retirement, with service to our communities and the planet as a priority, will we be healthy enough to be agents of transformation? In the spirit of the Serenity Prayer, although there are issues related to health and aging we may not be able to control, we have a great deal of agency in how we glorify God in our embodiment and how we practice wellness in our daily lives. Using our personal agency, rather than letting negative habits or the processes of aging take their course, awakens in our cells, organs, and whole being, the energies of creative transformation, empowering us to glorify God in our bodies so that we can share in God's vision of Shalom for our congregations, communities, nation, and the planet. We can have the discipline and courage to change what we once thought was impossible!

GLORIFYING GOD IN OUR BODIES

Many retired clergy discover that physical well-being is more a matter of choice than chance. Francis, a retired United Church of Christ pastor, living in an historic beach community, has discovered that in his mid-seventies that he has lost some of his physical energy. A widower, he has found that he typically has energy for only one significant activity each day. He has discovered that being single, he no longer has a companion for domestic chores and yard work and is spending time each decluttering the home he has lived in for three decades. He considers himself "blessed to have good health." Recently, he discovered a beautiful wooded path near his home and two or three times each week he goes on a ninety-minute hike. Francis notes that "hiking has given him more energy and has also enabled him to take off the weight that came with ministry and inactivity during retirement." Francis admits that in retirement his "besetting sin is sloth" and that the best way to counteract the laziness of "not have to do the daily tasks of ministry is to take time for exercise in a beautiful space." As I chatted with Francis, I found it difficult to believe that he is slothful: he is part of a classical-popular music group, participates in a retired pastors clergy group, actively involves himself in ongoing continuing education, and has several spiritual direction clients. Francis never imagined himself walking ninety minutes, period! Now these four-mile walks are central to his physical and spiritual disciples. "Out in nature, God is alive for me, and I come back noticing the wonder of my garden at home and the beauty of sea and sky!"

Cheryl also pushed beyond her self-imposed limits. She confesses, "I learned to swim late in life and never really liked it. I was afraid of water." This New England American Baptist pastor realized that she "needed to trust God and the water and my own skills." Wanting a low-impact exercise as a result of knee and foot issues related to arthritis, she enrolled in a beginning swim class at the local YMCA, advanced in her swimming ability and confidence. "Now I swim 45 minutes every morning. I feel stronger and my arthritis is better. I even do a little swimming at the local beach when the weather's warm. I call that a miracle!" she exclaims.

Now, at retirement age, but still at work, I recognize that I need to continue the healthy practices I have followed for over four decades and make changes to promote better health for the long haul. I have practiced meditation since my first year in college in 1970. First thing in the morning and at least once in the afternoon, I close my eyes and focus on my prayer word for fifteen to twenty minutes. My meditative practices began with Transcendental Meditation and have branched out to Centering Prayer, Walking Prayer, and Breath Prayer. For nearly thirty years, I have been a Reiki healing touch practitioner, including over two decades as a teacher–master. Most days of the week, I give myself a self-Reiki treatment, laying my hands on my energy centers, experiencing the calming flow of healing energy for ten to fifteen minutes. Medical research has found that in addition to the spiritual benefits of meditation and Reiki, both practices promote overall well-being and stress reduction and are factors in lowering blood pressure as well as pain relief. I was a daily jogger until by my late forties when I took up walking due to the physical stresses of running, what has been described as the "agony of de-feet!" Each morning, I "move with the spirit," walking two miles on the beaches and wooded neighborhoods of Cape Cod. Now, that I have found myself more robust weight-wise than is healthful, I try to take a second walk with my 90-pound Golden Doodle in the afternoon. I enjoy good food, and still snack when I am working around the house.

I must confess that I am a "work in progress" when it comes to diet and fluids. I am trying to be more conscious of my eating habits, drink more water, and practice portion control. Although I often fail in this endeavor, I realize that mindfulness is the first step toward a healthy lifestyle. I have come to realize the relationship between eating meat and environmental destruction. Our diets for this "small planet" have become ethical issues for many retired clergy. We recognize that eating more vegetables and fewer meat products reduces the release of methane gas in the atmosphere and may be a factor in protecting the "lungs of the planet," the Amazon rain forest!

Jan, a retired United Methodist pastor, now living in Florida, learned the importance of self-care after a heart attack scare. "When I was in the emergency room, I had a come to Jesus moment. I was forty pounds overweight, ate fast foods, had a personal relationship with my couch, and didn't exercise." Still committed to justice issues, this seventy-year-old pastor realized that healing the world meant healing herself. When we talked about the man at the pool (John 5), she confessed that the question "do you want to be healed?" convicted her of her unhealthy lifestyle? She also pondered, like the man at the pool, how badly she wanted to be healthy. "I might live another twenty years and I didn't want to live it with a walker! I wanted to be on the front lines not the sidelines in confronting injustice. So, I changed my life, so I could reach out to others. It's about stewardship. I needed to get back in shape so I could continue to work for justice."

Jan realized the importance of the airline instructions, "put on your oxygen mask first" prior to placing it on a vulnerable person next to you. "It took a while to change my habits. But I swore off red meat, except for a filet mignon with Roquefort sauce on special occasions, gave up candy, and cut down on carbs." For her, the greatest challenge was physical exercise. "I had to get off the couch and out in the world, not just to protest but to exercise. So, I joined a fitness club, worked with a trainer." Now, thirty pounds lighter and more energetic, Jan walks three miles daily in the Florida's fall, winter, and spring, and goes inside to exercise during Florida's summer heat. A social being, Jan joins a group of other women, many of whom share her progressive political views, for group walking three times a week. "We talk politics, plan outings and sometimes protests, and stay healthy. That's a winner with me."

Tom has followed a similar pattern of well-being so he can continue to be active in retirement. "My doctor diagnosed me with pulmonary issues and advised an exercise regimen to get me back on track. I go to the gym three to five time each week and the results have been amazing. I'm getting back my own energy and breathe more fully and deeply."

We can reverse the aging process through lifestyle decisions. Still, one of life's necessary losses is gradual physical diminishment despite our commitment to transformational dietary, activity, intellectual, and spiritual practices. A cross-country runner in college, Verne, a retired Reformed Church of America pastor from Michigan, confesses, "I'm discovering to my dismay that at least in my case, 65 most definitely isn't the new 50. It's strange to feel my physical and mental strength waning. Not disconcerting or disturbing, but certainly strange." While Verne laments the aging process that has shortened his runs through bucolic countryside near his home, he still drags his weary bones out for a three-mile run twice a week and walks an hour each day, often discussing the affairs of the day with his wife of forty years. "I may not be able to run and not be weary, as God says to Isaiah, but I can still run, joint pain and all, and for that I am grateful. I am determined not to rust out, but plan to keep fighting the good fight regardless of what the future brings." Never weary of doing good, Verne still crusades for justice, most recently for fair treatment for undocumented workers and pilgrims coming north from Central America. He has been active in refugee resettlement in Michigan. "I am convinced that despite feeling old some days, my exercise regimen gives me strength for struggle."

Carol retired in 2017, after closing the mid-western metropolitan area Disciples of Christ congregation she had pastored for over a decade. "They simply ran out of energy and money and needed to close, but I felt grief-stricken both at retiring earlier than I had hoped and being the last pastor of this church." Although physically active in her late sixties, mostly through water aerobics, Carol has, like Verne, faced some serious health crises—breast cancer, knee replacement, a broken wrist, and shoulder surgery, none of which could be connected with lifestyle issues, but rather the realities of chance and the wear and tear of the aging process. Still, Carol hopes to return to water aerobics after her shoulder heals. She and her husband love to travel and that requires being in shape. They are planning a month-long cruise that will take them to the Mediterranean and were packing for a weeklong holiday in New Orleans the day we spoke on the phone. Carol exemplifies the reality that when we do what we love, we can live vitally despite physical challenges.

In contrast, Karen, who retired at sixty after thirty years of urban and suburban ministry in the United Church of Christ, feels "better than ever" at sixty-three. When she retired, Karen felt exhausted from the rigors of a high-demand suburban church, where excellence was never good enough to satisfy either her congregation or herself. Karen confesses that during her three decades of ministry, "I never learned to take care of myself. I was always on the go, and never took time to replenish my spiritual or physical resources. By the time I retired, my well had run dry." Karen relates that "alcohol was the place I turned to relax after a hard day at church. A few glasses of wine every night helped me unwind and decompress, but by then I had nothing for my husband." Karen's salvation was entering a spiritually based program, aimed at persons with substance use disorders, "This Naked Mind," led by Annie Grace.[6] She was especially inspired by the program's emphasis on "how you can serve your community?"

Plagued by depression and unable to quit taking Prozac without serious side effects, Karen made a life-changing discovery. Her depression and the frequent migraine headaches that debilitated her were not primarily the result of depression or bipolarity but a brain disorder. A regimen of anti-seizure medication cured her of migraines as well as her depression and enabled her to go off Prozac without withdrawal symptoms. When I asked Karen about her exercise regimen, this former professional dancer and liturgical dance leader laughed and said, "taking care of my two year old granddaughter three days a week!" She also regularly practices yoga and has begun taking dance classes once more. After years of personal and professional struggles, Karen rejoices at her "amazing life" and "rebirth." Glowing with joy and gratitude, Karen affirms, "I'm a new person, less anxious, more centered, and more physically fit due to a combination of lifestyle changes, medication, exercise, and spiritual practices."

Each of these pastors recognizes the limits of life. They also recognize that overall well-being involves challenging preconceived limitations. Our bodies, minds, and spirits have wondrous recuperative powers. There is a movement toward health in our bodies just as there is a moral arc in the historical process. This energy of health is embodied in the lives of pastors and their spouses who got up off the coach and pushed away from the table to make healthy choices and then found themselves in better condition at seventy-five than forty.

Some retired clergy became race walkers, others competitive bicyclists, as a result of starting walking and racing clubs at Pilgrim Place, a faith-related retirement community in Claremont, California. They found that in moving their bodies and saying yes to physical health every other aspect of their lives improved. They discovered that despite the limitations inherent in the aging process and the social myths related to aging, they could explore ways of promoting physical health, exceeding what they had previously imagined. In the spirit of Isaiah's prophesy, they discovered that those who move as well as:

those who wait for the LORD shall renew their strength,
   they shall mount up with wings like eagles,
they shall run and not be weary,
   they shall walk and not faint. (Isaiah 40:31)

PATHWAYS TO JUBILEE

Health Examen

Most of us schedule a yearly physical to assess our overall physical well-being. Our health care provider checks various aspects of our health, ranging from weight and blood pressure to liver function and eyesight. Our physical, like our dental examinations, gives us the opportunity to change course in our lifestyle habits, adjusting behaviors to promote better health and wellness. As a result of my yearly physicals, I now take a medication for inherited as well as weight-related hypertension, drink less fruit juice and more water, and am more careful about carbohydrates. I am aware of my intake of sugar and red meat.

A similar process is employed in the Examen, a spiritual practice initiated by Ignatius of Loyola. In Ignatian spirituality, the Examen is a prayerful technique aimed at assessing your experience of God's presence in the course of your day, which includes the following:

1. Becoming aware of God's presence.
2. Reviewing the day with gratitude.
3. Paying attention to your emotional life and reaction to life situations.
4. Identifying one event or aspect of the day as an inspiration for prayer.

5. Looking toward tomorrow with gratitude for the possibility of personal transformation.

A Health Examen is similar and enables you to discern God's vision for your health in the present and the future and respond accordingly seeking God's Shalom in your physical life.

1. After a time of stillness, give thanks for your awesomely created body.
2. Review your current health with gratitude for God's blessings in your embodiment.
3. Noticing your overall well-being, quality of life, and relationship with your body.
4. Identify one aspect of your physical health as an inspiration to prayer and, possibly, creative transformation.
5. Looking toward the future with gratitude and resolve to move forward toward greater well-being.

Breath Prayer

On Easter night, Jesus breathed on his disciples and said, "Receive the Holy Spirit." Spirit is breath, whether it animates our individual spirits, the cells of our bodies, or respiratory system. Meditative spiritual practices, such as Centering Prayer and Transcendental Meditation, have been identified with stress reduction, pain relief, greater energy and creativity, and overall physical well-being. What nurtures the spirit also transforms the body. The body is inspired, and the soul embodied.

In breath prayer, we simply find a comfortable spot to sit for five to fifteen minutes. After a moment of silence, simply breathe, gently focusing your attention on each breath you take, inhaling and exhaling. Let this focus your mind on the ambient sources of wholeness and energy flowing through you every moment of the day. Let every breath become a prayer and as you join all creation in praising God (Psalm 148, 150). You may choose to employ a phrase to help you focus on your breath. One of my spiritual mentors Allan Armstrong Hunter counseled:

I breathe the spirit deeply in
And blow it gratefully out again.

Vietnamese Buddhist monk Thich Nhat Hanh has popularized the following breath prayer, which similar Hunter's breath prayer can be employed in sitting meditation and during your day.

Breathing in
I feel calm
Breathing out
I smile.

My own personal breath prayer mantra, or repeated phrase, goes as follows. When I inhale, I say "God's" and when I exhale, I say "Light" both to focus and to affirm that God's healing and loving light flows through me to the world with every breath.

Whenever you lose focus in the course of your meditation, simply bring your attention back to your breath, without any sense of judgment. For decades, I have advised seminarians and new pastors to adopt a spiritual practice I have used throughout my ministry: I pause a second before beginning their sermon. I close my eyes, take a deep healing and calming breath, before saying a short public prayer of illumination. In the course of the day, if you begin to feel anxious or angry, pause a moment to breathe deeply, perhaps using the prayer words cited above, to center your spirit and lower your anxiety so that any interactions may be spiritually centered, even if they involve righteous indignation in relationship to injustice, impoliteness, or uncivil behavior.

Walking Prayer

There are many pathways in walking prayer. Some persons walk slowly, almost at a snail's pace, breathing slowly and deliberately as a form of mindfulness meditation. Being somewhat utilitarian, I have devised a breath prayer that I employ as part of my morning walk each day. When I am at home, I walk about two to three miles from Craigville Beach to Covell's Beach and then through the historic Craigville neighborhood before returning to my staring point. I walk at a fast clip, and as I walk, I take deep breaths, focusing on each of the energy centers or chakras—the top of my head, my forehead, throat, heart, solar plexus, reproductive, and eliminative—beginning at the top of my head, going downward, and then returning to the top of my head. As I focus on each energy center, I say a prayer and make an affirmation:

Top of the head: God's wisdom flows through me to the world.
Forehead: Divine order and intelligence flow in and through me.
Throat: I speak God's healing words.
Heart: I am courageous and strong.

Solar Plexus: God's energy flows in and through me.
Reproductive: Divine creatively and Eros flow energize and flow through me.
Eliminative: I let go of the past and move forward toward God's future.

Often as I concentrate on each energy enter, I focus on someone in need of God's grace and healing or an issue I am dealing with. I experience God's enlightening, healing, and loving wisdom and energy flowing through me with each breath.

Explore Alternative Health Practices

Western medicine has been a gift from God. Many of us are alive today or live fully despite chronic illnesses through surgery, transplants, replacements, and medication. Still, there is much wisdom to be gained from complementary medicine. My life has flourished physically, mentally, and spiritually as a result of my daily practice of Reiki healing touch.[7] I give my wife a short Reiki healing touch treatment every night as we prepare for sleep. Kate claims that it has been an essential factor in her well-being.

Complementary medicine and health practices can take many forms: yoga, Tai Chi, Qigong, massage, therapeutic touch, as well as homeopathy and other integrative medical practices. In concert with an open-minded physician, you may decide to explore one of these healing techniques in response to chronic illness or promote ongoing physical well-being. We can give thanks for better living through chemistry. We can also rejoice in better living through God's healing energy. Both are gifts from the one whose ministry sought abundant life for us and all creation.

A Prayer for the Pathway: Embodied God, your word is made flesh in Jesus and in all creation. Your healing and loving light shines in all things. I thank you for the wonder of the universe and the wonder of my being, body, mind, spirit, and relationships. Inspire and encourage me to live with health and vitality. Help me to choose healthy habits so that I might serve you with gratitude, energy, and wisdom. In Christ's Name. Amen.

NOTES

1. Gwen Wagstrom Halas, *Clergy, Retirement, and Wholeness: Looking Forward to the Third Age* (Herndon, VA: Alban Institute, 2005).

2. Ibid., 15.

3. Duke Clergy Health Initiative, "Summary Report: 2014 Statewide Survey of United Methodist Clergy in North Carolina," 18–19. https://divinity.duke.edu/sites/divinity.duke.edu/files/documents/chi/2014%20Summary%20Report%20-%20

CHI%20Statewide%20Survey%20of%20United%20Methodist%20Clergy%20in%20North%20Carolina%20-%20web.pdf

4. Ibid., 16.

5. Stephanie Paulsell, *Honoring the Body: Meditations on a Christian Practice* (San Francisco: Jossey-Bass, 2002), 79.

6. https://thisnakedmind.com/

7. Bruce Epperly, *The Energy of Love: Reiki Healing Touch and Christian Healing* (Gonzales, FL: Energion Publications, 2017) and Bruce Epperly and Katherine Epperly, *Reiki Healing Touch and the Way of Jesus* (Kelowna, BC: Northstone Books, 2005).

Chapter 5

Bricks, Mortar, Money, and Movement

But strive first for the kingdom of God and his righteousness, and all these things will be given to you as well. (Matthew 6:33)

One of the anchor scriptures of this book and my own spiritual life is Jacob's exclamation after awakening from the dream of a ladder of angels. Awe-filled, the Hebraic patriarch exclaims, "God was in this place and I did not know it" (Genesis 28:16). This place of discovery, Beth-El, is everywhere. While each one of us has our own holy places, "thin places," where heaven and earth meet, inspiring and transforming Celtic pilgrims, every place can become a thin place where we can experience divine inspiration and guidance. God addresses us in every encounter. God whispers in the wind and God is present guiding us in our plans for retirement and congregational budget meetings. We often do not recognize God in the challenges, conflicts, and uncertainties, of congregational and personal business but recognized or not, God is here, guiding, inspiring, enlightening, and provoking change. After the fact, we often discover that God has made a way where we had perceived no way!

The Building and Grounds Team, aka the Trustees of South Congregational Church, Centerville, Massachusetts, are familiar with my assertion that "Brick and Mortar" are holy, too. Repairs, heating bills, and capital campaigns are not just about money, safety, and aesthetics; they are also about providing a home for spiritual seekers, a place for children to discover their vocations, a catalyst for service and social concern, and a community to nurture spiritual transformation in every season of life.

What we do with our treasures is a spiritual matter, reflecting our values and relationships. Amos connects social injustice and income inequality with a famine of hearing the world of God. Jesus tells of a man who congratulates himself on a bountiful harvest, builds a great barn, and dies the night of its completion. Our attitudes toward our treasure open or close the door to God's presence in our lives.

Writing this book has been a spiritual journey for me, involving reviewing the past, assessing the present, and envisioning the future. I have explored youthful traumas, professional successes and failures, relational joys and challenges, pondered the impact of my pastor-father's ministry on my own ministerial expectations and achievements, and taken a long hard look at the impact of my decisions and dreams on my retirement and aging. In my spiritual life review, one of the most painful and challenging areas has been looking at my attitudes toward money and financial security. Although my wife and I look forward to a fairly comfortable retirement due to good pension plans (the United Church of Christ and TIAA/CREF as well as Social Security) and have financially benefitted from inheriting property from our parents and selling our own homes during boom times, my childhood sense of financial insecurity surfaces from time to time. I have worked hard spiritualty to live by abundance rather scarcity in terms of my attitudes toward money. Today, I live by the affirmation, "I have all the time, talent, and treasure I need to live joyfully, give generously, and serve God" as an antidote to feelings of scarcity.

My attitudes toward money were formed in childhood by parents' financial insecurities. My mother and father came from modest means and lived as young adults through the depression. My maternal grandfather apparently was a jack of all trades, who supported his family from paycheck to paycheck. My father's family members were farmers, never owning their property, and eking out just enough income to get by. When my grandfather died during the depression, my father's responsibility was to farm the land and support his mother. My father was liberated from farm life by World War II. Although he was over thirty, he served in the Pacific theater, was given the rank of Second Lieutenant, and settled in California after the war. A beneficiary of the GI Bill, my father went to college at the University of California and seminary at the Berkeley Baptist Divinity School (now American Baptist Seminary of the West) and served for the next dozen years in small-town congregations, where my brother and I grew up as children of the parsonage.

When I was eleven, my father was terminated from his congregational position at the American Baptist Church in King City, California. The causes of termination were always a mystery to me. One story suggested that after eleven years in the same church, my father wore out his welcome, being a moderate in a conservative congregation, who reached out to the Mexican bracero, farmworker community, and allowed peace pilgrims and migrants to sleep in our garage and in the church. We moved to San Jose, a mushrooming city south of San Francisco, where my dad fell from prominence as a small-town pastor to unemployment and then work as a security guard and magazine salesman, prior to securing a chaplaincy position at an alcoholic rehabilitation center. Our family was close to poverty at the time, and even received food baskets from benevolent organizations. Summoning up all the pluck she had, my mother returned to college and elementary school teaching, receiving her California state teaching certificate in her mid-forties. Despite depression and obsessive thinking, my mother was an early childhood educator for the next twenty years. According to a confession made by my mother to her now grown-up son, my father even considered suicide, believing that he would be more valuable dead than alive!

I make this confession as part of my own spiritual life review and the impact scarcity thinking has had on my own attitudes toward money and financial security. Obviously, attitudes toward money have been a source of conflict with my wife, raised as upper middle class, always having enough, and traveling overseas as a child nearly every summer. Her family was not wealthy, but it had the resources to live well, giving my wife a sense that regardless of how much money she spent, there would always be more in the future. Over the years, I have learned to trust the biblical affirmation, "God will satisfy all your needs according to God's riches in glory in Christ Jesus" (Philippians 4:19, AP). The future of my own professional life has been twice uncertain when, despite the widely recognized success and high quality of my work, I was downsized from chaplaincy and administrative positions from Georgetown University after seventeen years and Lancaster Theological Seminary after nearly a decade of service. I found myself in the same spot at forty-seven and fifty-eight that my father did in his early fifties. Although I felt the same financial and professional insecurity as my father did, I was determined to choose differently, explore new possibilities, and see my professional dead ends as open doors. In each case, after facing my fears and insecurities, I was able to move forward personally and professionally, discovering a way where initially I saw no way!

Now anticipating retirement in the next few years, I have experienced a conversion of heart when it comes to finances. My wife and I have planned well, lived abundantly and within our means, and have the resources, barring another national economic collapse, to enjoy retirement with sufficient financial largesse to travel, live comfortably, volunteer in the community, and maintain a high level of giving to the church, political organizations, and programs responding to poverty and disease. We will need to be careful financially. I hopefully will continue to do some part-time teaching and occasional sabbatical replacement pastoral ministry and preaching well into my seventies. Yet, we are already imagining creative adventures emerging from more spacious schedules and the wherewithal to pursue them. Although I feel grateful for my own financial situation, I am distressed that in our wealthy nation, nearly 40 percent of households have less than US$400 in savings and would be put at financial risk by a health crisis, damage to their home, automobile repair, or work disruption due to a pandemic. Sadly, many of these Americans at risk are clergy and retired clergy, like Sam, now seventy-three, who confided that "I still can't retire yet. I need at least or two more interims to get me through financially. Maybe I'll work till I drop dead!" A second-career pastor, Sam has been faithful to the gospel in small-town ministry for the past thirty years. He and his wife used their IRA's and life savings for him to attend seminary and now they must work well into their seventies to catch up financially. Again, Sam laments, "I love the ministry. I feel like can help these small churches out. But I'm getting tired. I may only have a few good years left when I finally retire in my late seventies, and then where will we live. We don't own a home and still don't have a lot in savings, though our social security comes monthly and our pensions are recovering. I'm trusting God, but I often feel nervous when I look toward the future."

Sam's concerns are echoed by Sharon, a mid-western Disciples of Christ pastor, sixty-nine and single for the past decade. "I still have fire in my heart and love preaching, but I'm running out of steam. I figure I need a couple more years of paychecks to be in shape to retire. I live in the church's parsonage and haven't saved enough to buy a home. I am fortunate that both of my daughters have invited me to live with them. Otherwise I don't know what I would do."

MONEY MATTERS

In a recent conversation with members of the Pension Board of the United Church of Christ, I was reminded of the importance of financial stability in overall well-being. While finances are not at the top of Maslow's hierarchy of values, the realities of health and money shape our decision-making, vision of possibilities, and day-to-day stress, and widen or constrict our imaginations. Financial stability—the ability to provide your basic survival needs as well as creative ventures—like good health is seldom noticed unless we are forced to struggle to make ends meet in terms of housing, health care, food, and transportation. As one UCC Pension Board member noted, "a common denominator for thriving in retirement is financial wellness. A good financial foundation undergirds our physical well-being, overall happiness, and ability to serve the community." Not worried about next month's living expenses or an unexpected home repair or medication, retired pastors can live abundantly and generously, sharing their time, talent, and treasure for the glory of God and the creative transformation of their communities and the planet. They do not have to take one more lackluster interim, in some cases, marshalling just enough energy to make it another few years before diminishment and death!

Most pastors today can give thanks for denominational pioneers who established pension and health plans to promote clergy well-being across a lifetime. Virtually every denominational pension board offers pre-retirement seminars and advises pastors that retirement planning should begin with your first ministerial call, regardless of age. Sometimes pre-retirement seminars provide essential information that paves the way to a financially secure future. As a pension plan representative asserted, "Many pastors are not aware of what's available to them in retirement, especially the fact that they can, as they did during their ministries, deduct their housing expenses from their overall income. Although you should always check with your pension plan or financial advisor, this deduction can save several thousand dollars from federal and many state income taxes."

Recognizing that a healthy retirement involves more than financial stability, one pensions officer stated that well-being is ultimately related to questions such as: "What is the purpose of this new phase in your life? What are you retiring to? What will your future look like, when you retire, in five years, in ten years, and in twenty years and beyond?" Without meaning, money gives little solace as consider new future possibilities. Still, money promotes meaning insofar as it gives us the largesse to pursue our dreams and explore new horizons of service, knowing we have the financial resources to be generous with our time, talent, and treasure in retirement.

ABUNDANT LIVING

As Jesus' mission statement, recorded in John 10:10, asserts, God wants us to live abundantly in body, mind, and spirit. While scripture does not advocate the pursuit of wealth as a life goal or support the theological materialism of the "prosperity gospel," the biblical tradition identifies well-being with adequate food, shelter, and income. The prophets railed against the income disparity between the poor and wealthy. The Jerusalem church advocated a type of spiritual communalism in which everyone sold their property and placed in a common pool to ensure the physical well-being of every member (Acts 2:42–7, 4:32–7). Jesus was profoundly concerned with physical health, as evidenced by his healing ministry, and adequate nutrition, as revealed in Jesus' miraculous transformation of a few loaves of bread into banquet for thousands. Jesus enjoyed a good meal, saw table fellowship as holy, and rejoiced in providing adult beverages for a wedding celebration.

Despite their attempts to live simply and responsibly, for many pastors, retirement may. be a financial challenge. According to one commentator, "many [pastors] find themselves in a financial quandary as they approach or reach retirement, squeezed by challenges that sometimes exceed those of other professionals. Often lacking home equity and a pension, some are struggling to get by and others are staying on the job longer."[1]

This is surely true for pastors in their seventies who take one interim after another, serving as placeholders rather than transformers for struggling congregations. According to Bert White, a retired United Methodist pastor and lecturer at Boston University, "The root of the problem is not just limited pay or retirement compensation . . . It's a lack of financial literacy among people who really need to take control of their personal finances or risk ending up in dire straits." White adds, "Clergy are so focused on the hereafter, but we should know more about planning for life after work."

While I agree with much of what White notes, I see the issue of clergy financial well-being as more nuanced both theologically and practically. On the one hand, many clergy have a challenging time advocating for their own needs. Clergy are supposed to be persons for others, pouring themselves out for the poor and vulnerable, and they think little of themselves. Like today's public schoolteachers, many pay for church programs out of their own pockets and give generously beyond the church budget to persons in need of food and housing. I recall one Central Pennsylvania pastor stating that he put all his wedding honorariums in a savings account, and then sent a check to each couple on their first wedding anniversary with the counsel to "go out and have a great meal together." While I appreciate his sentiments, I wonder how many "great meals" or holidays his wife missed because of this modestly paid, small-town pastor's generosity to other couples.

As pastors, we are called to love others as ourselves, but Jesus' counsel applies to the others in our family as well as people in our community. It also calls us to love ourselves congruent with our support of others and the common good. Further, many congregations can provide only as much compensation as their budget allows to their pastors. As another Central Pennsylvania pastor confesses, "I'm afraid to ask for more. My income and benefits match or exceed most of our members, and my salary and benefits package is almost 40% of the church budget, which is always in the red." Ironically, many suburban pastors are well paid in terms of dollar amounts in relationship to their rural colleagues, but their salaries are well below their congregants with similar education and expertise. As one metropolitan Boston pastor shared with me, "My total package, including retirement, social security offset, and health insurance, is close to $140,000, and I feel blessed. But entry level for housing in our community is nearly $750,000, and we are in the lower third of income our congregation. My husband and I both have to work to make ends meet."

While his package is exceptional in terms of national averages, and would be the envy of many pastors, so is the cost of living in his community! Staying in the same community after they retire is not an option for many suburban pastors, if they have been unable to purchase a home in the area where they pastored.

In reflecting on the financial challenges some pastors face, it is important to note other factors that shape financial stability in retirement: the financial support pastors receive from the churches they pastor, where they pastor (urban, suburban, rural, small town), property values, and the cost of living of the place where they retire, as well as issues of gender and age of entry into ministry. Many second-career pastors deplete their savings, go into debt, and forego years of retirement contributions as they prepare for ministry, much of which will occur in small, cash-strapped congregations. Moreover, both married and single women often receive less compensation than their male counterparts or, as in my wife's case, she chose to work part-time during our son's formative years. I will add that we chose for four years to share a 1.5 full-time equivalent position as university chaplains so that both of us would be present for our son's school programs and extracurricular activities. Although we do not regret our decision, we estimate that it cost us over US$100,000 in retirement funds during her working career, not to mention savings and additional mortgage payments.

Still, financial planning is key at every stage of ministry. While we may not be able to say with John Wesley, "make all you can," we can aspire to "save all you can and give all you can."

In recalling the "sagely" advice he received from his bishop, Bert White notes that when he was being ordained forty years ago, his bishop told him "Bert, you won't ever make any money as a clergyman but you'll always have a great retirement plan." White replied, "Oh, really?" To which the bishop responded, "Yeah, it's eternal life after you die."[2] Still, for many retired pastors, there is a long time between here and eternity and they may struggle to make ends meet, if their pensions and social security are inadequate.

Andrew, a retired Disciples of Christ pastor, living in a Southern California suburb, notes that although he and wife live in their own home, their respective pensions and social security do not measure up to their salaries at the time of their retirement. "Perhaps we could have planned better or I could have worked a few years more," Andrew, now age seventy-five, reflects, "But sixty seven seemed the right time for me. The problem was that my wife worked part-time through much of our marriage, stayed home when our children were young, and I spent most of my career in small town California and Oregon churches whose salaries and pension contributions were sufficient, but still modest. We are blessed compared to most people of the world. We have some savings and can cover our bills, but we don't have much extra to travel to the East Coast to see our children and grandchildren."

If a part-time interim ministry was available in the area, Andrew admits, "I might just put my name in. I still have the energy and skills, and it would take the edge of off things financially."

In contrast, Sue and Steve are doing quite well financially. A pioneering woman in ministry, Sue recently retired after forty years in full-time ministry, the last five as an interim at multiple-staff congregations and at the presbytery level. Steve, her husband of nearly fifty years, also recently retired from his faculty position at a local community college. Both have good pensions through the church and the college retirement plan (TIAA/CREF). Sue gratefully acknowledges that "we are among the lucky ones. With four decades each on good retirement plans, professional stability that enabled to live and pay for the home we've lived in for thirty years, we have more than enough to get by. In fact, we have money left over many months. We've kept up our giving to the local and national church and to political causes. We have the freedom to volunteer and travel with Habitat for Humanity and the national church."

Politically involved, at the time of our conversation, Sue and Steve were looking forward to traveling to Iowa and New Hampshire in 2020 to campaign for their Democratic candidate of choice and plan to be campaigning in November 2020 as well. Sue reflects on her current life with a sense of gratitude for her largesse, "While I don't feel guilty, I know that most of the world and many of my peers in ministry are not as fortunate as I am. We aren't wealthy but we are doing well compared to most Americans and we take for granted what many would consider luxuries. This has challenged us to be generous right now, knowing as the hymn says, 'We give thee but thine own' and to support the causes that are important to us through planned giving."

MOVING WITH THE SPIRIT AND SACRAMENTAL STABILITY

One of the great joys of a lifetime of seminary and graduate school teaching is seeing my former students become talented and effective pastors, chaplains, and administrators. I am delighted to hear how their seminary experiences prepared them for professional adventures. Now retired to New Hampshire, Wendy, a second-career United Church of Christ pastor and student of mine at Lancaster Theological Seminary, is grateful for her pilgrimage from Pennsylvania to New England. As we shared seminary stories and memories from her first years in ministry, Wendy expressed her gratitude for the opportunity to live near her grandchildren. "When my husband and I retired, we had a choice to make. Throughout my ministry, we regularly commuted to New Hampshire and Oregon where our children lived. We wanted to live near them, but where? We finally decided to settle in New Hampshire where two of our three children lived. We go to Oregon a couple times a year but being near our four New Hampshire grandchildren swayed or decision."

Wendy and her husband found a home near one of New Hampshire's picturesque lakes, two miles from one child and forty miles from the other. "We have become taxi drivers and youth sports enthusiasts for our grandchildren—with softball, piano, dog sled, and soccer, not to mention our time on the water. We have a great life here. When it comes down to it, it's all about family." Although her own pension is modest, Wendy is grateful for the largesse of her husband's pension that enables them to live well on the lake and travel regularly to the West Coast. Still, Wendy notes that retirement means the opportunity to "live more simply. We don't need new clothes. We focus our income on our children and grandchildren. That's our stewardship these days, helping our children enjoy their lives and grow up to be adults who make a difference."

Carol and her husband chose to accept a call in a metropolitan area to be near their parents. Although their parents are now deceased, they plan to bloom where they are planted. One child lives two miles away, and the other forty miles away. Now in her late sixties, Carol is hoping for a grandchild, but in the meantime, she delights in "being able to visit the kids and have them over at our house. Our life now revolves around travel and family. Until the next step of my journey is revealed to me, this is truly a great life!"

Having a parsonage can be both a blessing and a curse. On the one hand, parsonages enable congregations to provide adequate compensation, especially in metropolitan areas where housing prices make it difficult for pastors to purchase their homes. They also lower the bottom line in congregational budgets. On the other hand, pastors who spend their ministerial careers living in parsonages may have difficulties finding adequate housing at retirement, if they have not put away sufficient savings or lack the retirement income for mortgage payments.

When Steve was called to pastor a large suburban church, he gladly moved into the congregation's spacious and attractive parsonage. He needed time to get his bearings in a new congregation and decide whether this would be final full-time pastoral appointment. Five years into a fifteen-year call, he sat down with the church board to share his desire to purchase his first home at age fifty-seven. "The church leadership was supportive. They all owned their homes and valued home ownership. They recognized that our children had left home, married, and were raising families in the metropolitan area. They knew that I wanted to stay close to my children and the first of what ended up being four grandchildren. They approved my request, and two years later

I purchased my home five miles from the church." Today, Steve and his wife say that this was one of the best decisions they ever made. Three years after retiring and now seventy, Steve reports that "We live midway between our children and grandchildren. Being just twenty minutes away gives an opportunity to be close but not too close. We see a grandchild at least five days a week for sports, childcare, and sleepovers. We give our sons and our wives a chance to get away for a date on a regular basis."

Both Steve and his wife Sue have good pensions from ministry and teaching, respectively, and have the resources to travel, do home improvements, and generously support their church and other benevolences.

Susan spent twenty years living in her Boston congregation's parsonage before purchasing a vacation home on Cape Cod. She and her husband had the resources to purchase the home and make home improvements before moving in for good when they retired. They had enjoyed their Cape Cod home, a mile from the beach, for Friday–Saturday escapes and summer holidays, and now they are delighted to be near the beach, cranberry bogs, and their local church. They pinch pennies at times to support their children's and grandchildren's needs, but they are grateful to have enough financial largesse to be generous to the community in terms of time and talent.

Jack, another East Coast pastor and his life, fell in love with Maine, spending six to eight weeks yearly at their home walking distance from a pond and a short drive from the beach. Having a parsonage was a blessing for this two-income professional couple. Their salaries, combined with the financial benefits of not paying a mortgage in an affluent suburban neighborhood, enabled them to have the largesse to purchase a lovely retirement home three hours from their son and grandchild in the Boston area. After several years of retirement, Jack and his wife chose to uproot themselves one more time. Now in their late seventies, they relocated to a lovely, graduated care retirement community, less than an hour from their Boston family. "We are grateful for the counsel of a good financial planner and the opportunity to purchase a home in paradise. Now we look forward to aging in place, near family, and being able to move to assisted living or nursing care if we are unable to take care of ourselves. We don't like to think of that possibility, but we need to plan for sickness as well as health."

At sixty-five, it was time for Tom to retire from full-time ministry. Married for over forty years, and without children, Tom and Susan pondered long and hard where they would live in retirement. They wanted to travel. Living the Northeast, they were also tired of snow shoveling and home maintenance. After much soul-searching, they decided to settle in a New England retirement village with graduated care. Tom recognizes that "you need to have sufficient funds to move in and to pay monthly fees. But, once you're in, you're there for life." Tom and Susan enjoy the built-in community and have become active in the community. Tom shares his computer and information technology skills with fellow residents, helping them with software problems and installing programs. "I usually spend a few hours a week providing support for my fellow residents. It's great to use my skills and to be of service." Currently, Tom is not interested in interim ministry, but was glad on a recent snow day to conduct services in the retirement community for those who could not make it to their local congregations. "It was fulfilling to be preacher once more. I'm not sure I want to preach weekly. But I love preaching and liturgy and want to share my gifts with local congregations on an occasional basis."

In contrast, Ted and his wife Carolyn struggled to find a home when he retired at seventy after forty-five years in small town and county seat churches. "I had to stick it out to my early seventies to garner the resources to find a comfortable home for the two of us. My last congregation was in a town of three thousand with few medical services. We knew we couldn't stay. We would get in the way of the new pastor, but we wondered where we could afford to move. Our children lived on both coasts, and we couldn't afford housing in either Philadelphia or San Francisco. We finally chose a small ranch house west of Lancaster, Pennsylvania."

Ted and Carolyn live modestly and can only afford to fly to California once a year, with their son's financial help. In their late seventies, they are glad to be only seventy miles from their son, living in the Philadelphia suburbs. The size of Lancaster, Pennsylvania, gives them opportunities for entertainment, culture, and service they would not have experienced had they remained in small town. Newcomers to the area, they had many churches to choose from, without boundary issues, and soon found themselves involved in the hands-on as well as political aspects of immigration and refugee resettlement.

PILGRIMS BUT NOT STRANGERS

Pilgrim Place is tucked in a tree-lined community in the idyllic college town of Claremont, California, where I attended graduate school. For the past several years, my wife and I have been encouraged to apply for residence at this intentional graduated care community, populated by ministers, professors, missionaries, and a small number of religiously active and socially committed retired professionals. Virtually every year since my theological mentor John Cobb retired to Pilgrim Place, I have enjoyed lunch at the spacious dining hall, catching up with Professor Cobb as well as other former professors and pastors who influenced my ministry and academic life. Pilgrim Place's website describes the community in terms of growth and social consciousness.

From its inception, members of Pilgrim Place community have reached out and demonstrated that elders are a rich spiritual resource. Peace, justice, and sustainability are topics that are woven into the fabric of Pilgrim Place. Social change and how it occurs is part of our daily conversation.[3]

Pilgrim place seeks to foster a "vibrant and inclusive senior community, committed to justice, peace, and care for the earth." As I walked the community's grounds, ate at the dining hall with two groups of residents, and met several "pilgrims," as they call themselves, at a local bistro for drinks, I encountered authors, professors, social activists, and contemplatives, all committed to social transformation and planetary healing. Life is full at Pilgrim Place. It is an intentional community, almost monastic, with individual residences.

Every Friday, a group of pilgrims gather to demonstrate on a major Claremont thoroughfare, protesting endless war, climate denial by government leaders, impeachment results, immigration policy, racism, and homophobia. True to their convictions, the community is selling a plot of land at the edge of the campus to be dedicated to affordable housing in response to California's homeless and housing crisis.

Activism of every variety can be found at Pilgrim Place. As one resident averred, "You retire to some places for the location. At Pilgrim Place, you come for the people." Residents are challenged to grow spiritually, intellectually, artistically, and politically through the organic gardens, worship and meditation groups, the art studio, book groups, theological reflection, and social activism. "It's a retirement community where you don't retire but continue to explore your own gifts and discover new ones," another resident asserted. Open and inclusive, Pilgrim Place has become a haven for gay and lesbian persons and is now exploring what it would mean to have transgendered residents. "It's a safe place for the LGBTQ community. We can be ourselves here at Pilgrim Place. We don't have to go back into the closet as some people do at other retirement communities," a community resident shared over drinks with several other gay and lesbian residents.

Like many retirement communities, Pilgrim Place requires its members to share lunch with one another daily. What is unique about lunches at Pilgrim Place is that members must play a game of musical chairs at the community meal. Each day seat assignments change so that persons can widen their circle of friends and acquaintances. Each day's meal is punctuated by prayer, announcements of political, religious, and cultural activities, and introduction of visitors, which often goes on for ten to fifteen minutes. During one of the lunches I attended, a group of college students from the East Coast were introduced. They had come to Pilgrim Place to speak with members about spirituality and sustainability. Friends from across the globe were also welcomed into the community.

Pilgrim Place is an environment where you can push your personal limits. Committed to nurture body as well as spirit, pilgrims have initiated world-class senior fast-walking and cycling teams. "We have limits as we grow older, but we don't know them till we try. I didn't think I could be a fast walker, but I've exceeded every expectation and I'm healthier than I was at 55," noted one fast-walking team member, now in her mid-seventies.

A community filled with pastors, religious workers, and missionaries makes pastoral care a priority with members going to medical appointments with one another, visiting at the assisted care and nursing facilities, and facilitating grief groups. Grief, aging, and death are real at Pilgrim Place, and they cannot be denied. Many of those with whom I spoke found the realities of mortality a source of self-awareness rather than fear. While most of the pilgrims with whom I spoke are agnostic about the nature of the afterlife, all are committed to living joyfully in the Place. When one member asserted, "I love life," his companions around the table all nodded their heads. In response to my query about what gives them hope, pilgrims expressed their concern about the future and the deathful behaviors of the current White House and held their concerns in tension with their hope "in activist youth" such as the Parkland students and Greta Thunberg and "intergenerational partnerships with students from the Claremont Colleges." Community is real at Pilgrim Place, and jubilation describes most residents' retirement. I must admit that my wife and I would consider moving to Pilgrim Place in our seventies if we were not already committed to our son and his family.

Brick and mortar, and the communities in which we live are holy. Remembering that God is with us in the challenges of finances and house-holding along with planning for the future serves as the foundation for retired clergy to pursue new adventures in service and spiritual growth. None of the pastors with whom I spoke are wealthy and a few have to watch every cent or take on part-time pastoral tasks such as supply preaching to deal with unexpected expense or take trips, and none of them regret saying "yes" to God's call. All of them saw the financial rewards of ministry as insignificant compared with the opportunity to serve God and be agents of healing and meaning in persons' lives. All of them believed that God still had a future and a hope planned for them and wanted to use their resources in time, talent, and treasure to fulfill their vocation as God's companions in healing the earth.

PATHWAYS TO JUBILEE

Abundance and Scarcity

Many members of the "greatest generation," the builders who lived the Depression and World War II, describe their family economics during the

Depression years with the phrase, "We weren't poor. We just didn't have any money." People like my wife's grandmother and my father, living on modest means, without batting an eye, shared with people less fortunate than themselves. My wife's grandmother, a widow with teenage daughters, rented out rooms in their Shaker Heights, Ohio, home to makes ends meet, but never evicted a boarder for inability to pay. My father and his neighbors always had enough to go around for another place at the table, when an unemployed man came to the door, though they usually asked him to do a few chores around the farm as a way of maintaining self-respect.

One of Jesus' mission statements, recorded in scripture, is "I came that they might have life, and have it abundantly" (John 10:10). Abundance and scarcity are a matter of attitude as well as finances. When we live with scarcity, we never have enough time, treasure, or talent. We envy others and try to undermine their successes for our ego-gratification. We believe ourselves to be poor even when we have a million dollars set aside in pensions or own a chain of hotels. We are always on the run and never in the moment. Living by scarcity cuts us off from the bountiful resources that are always available to us if we open hearts and hands to give and receive. Nations can live by scarcity, forgetting their bounty as they try to protect a way of life that no longer exists.

As I write these words in 2020, our nation is facing an influx of pilgrims from South America. Despite the efforts of government workers, immigrants are living in unsanitary and crowded conditions and receiving unhealthy food—in the wealthiest country on the planet! Regardless of your view on immigration, our leaders' complaint that we do not have any resources to help them or their nations of origin betrays a sense of scarcity, when we have more than enough for weapons systems and subsidies for the wealthy. As groups confronting global hunger and poverty—many of them led by retired clergy—in our own country assert, there is more than enough food and social support to go around if decide to share the bounty we have.

One of my favorite stories recounts the generosity of the boy whose five loaves and two fishes feed a multitude. When Jesus asks his disciples to feed the thousands gathered to hear his message, they are overwhelmed by the enormity of the task. They protest "we don't have enough money to buy meals for a group this size." No doubt the call goes out to the crowd, but no one admits to having brought any food to the event. Then, a boy—and boys can be hungry!—shows up with five loaves and two fish, and Jesus transforms his modest lunch into a banquet for thousands. Jesus and the young boy saw abundance, while others saw scarcity. Living by prayerful abundance, Jesus multiplied what little had into a feast. In my imagination, without discounting Jesus' ability to multiply the loaves and fish, I visualize the crowd witnessing the boy's generosity and then, convicted of their scarcity thinking and selfish behavior, pull out their knapsacks to create potluck dinner for the assembled multitudes.

Affirmative Faith

As the first part of a spiritual Examen, ponder your attitude toward life. Do you see the world and your life as abundant and connected with resources you can tap into or do you see the world and your life in terms of scarcity and isolation? If you see the world through the eyes of scarcity, what practices might enable you to experience God's abundance more fully?

In my own process of spiritual transformation, the use of affirmations has broadened my vision, expanded my imagination, and changed my behaviors. Affirmations begin at the conscious mind but over time become the conscious and unconscious lens through which we view our resources and the events of our lives. If you hold onto an affirmation for few minutes or repeat it several times a day, especially when you are tempted to fall back into habitual behaviors, you will discover new insights and ways of approaching your life. You will begin, as the adage says, to see the glass as half full rather than half empty. As respond to my own tendency toward scarcity thinking, I have claimed abundance by affirmations such as:

My God will satisfy all my needs according to his riches
   in glory in Christ Jesus. (Philippians 4:19)
I can do all things through him who strengthens me. (Philippians 4:13)
God wants me to have abundant life. (John 10:10)
Nothing in life can separate me from the love of God. (Romans 8:38–9)

I also use non-scriptural affirmations such as:

I have all the time, talent, and treasure to live faithfully,
   glorify God, and serve my neighbor.
I am grateful for my abundance and generously share with others.
I give and receive blessings in every situation.
God's generosity flows through me to respond to strangers and neighbors.

Financial Examen

Brick and mortar are holy. Jesus and the prophets claimed that our attitudes toward our resources were profoundly spiritual and reflected our willingness to trust God and reach out to our neighbor. Wealth and poverty are spiritual issues, inviting us to live prayerfully and simply so that others might simply live. An Examen of finances follows the same pattern as a spiritual Examen, with the focus on how we view our financial resources in terms of our relationship with God and our neighbors.

In the spirit of last chapter's Health Examen, this Examen involves prayerfully assessing your experience of God's presence in the course of your day. A traditional Examen has the following components:

1. Becoming aware of God's presence in your life.
2. Reviewing the day with gratitude.
3. Paying attention to your emotional life and reaction to life situations.
4. Identifying the events of your day as an inspiration for prayer, noting the quality of your relationship to God in these events.
5. Looking toward tomorrow with gratitude for the possibility of personal transformation.

A Financial Examen enables you to discern God's vision for your financial affairs in the present and the future, moving you from scarcity to abundance and isolation to community.

1. After a time of stillness, give thanks for the wondrous world that sustains you and your family in body, mind, and spirit. Affirm generous interdependence of life, grounded in God's graceful providence.
2. Review your current financial situation with gratitude for God's blessings in terms of time, talent, and treasure. (As a prelude to this you might choose to consult a financial adviser, who will help you review your assets. This is especially helpful as you prepare for retirement. Most denominational pension funds provide resources for financial advice.)
3. Noticing your overall attitudes toward your current and future financial situation.
4. Identify one aspect of your financial life as an inspiration to prayer and, possibly, creative transformation.
5. Look toward the future with gratitude and resolve to move forward toward greater financial stability and generosity. (Grounded in an accurate assessment of your financial situation and earning possibilities, you may choose to embody the spirit of John Wesley's financial counsel: "*Make all you can, save all you can*, give all you can.")

Your Ideal Home

Home is where the heart is, so the saying goes. Our homes are, at their best, sacred spaces where we experience the love of friends and family. Our homes are retreats from the busyness of life and inspirations to go out into the world sharing God's good news. In this imaginative exercise, visualize where you would like to live and with whom you wish to share your life.

Begin with a time of quiet prayer, breathing deeply the resources of God's abundant universe. Given your resources and life situation, visualize the home you would like to live in. What are its dimensions? Furniture? Environment? Where is its location? With whom would you like to share your home on a daily or regular basis? In what ways will you make your home a place of hospitality for all who enter?

Becoming more concrete, if you are not currently in your ideal home, what do you need to do to incarnate this ideal vision in your current home or another for yourself and your loved ones?

Give thanks for God's guidance and support and ask God to give you wisdom and energy to achieve your ideal home.

A Prayer for the Pathway. Holy God, open my eyes and awaken my spirit. Help me experience God in this place, wherever I find myself. Let me live by abundance, enjoying sufficient largesse to live comfortably and share generously with those around me. Let me remember the "least of these," seeing all people as God's children and seeing my resources as ways to experience God and become God's companion in healing the world. In Christ's name. Amen.

NOTES

1. David Carpenter, "Many Clergy Not Ready for Retirement" (June 6, 2010). http://www.nbcnews.com/id/37493788/ns/business-your_retirement/t/many-clergy -not-ready-retirement/#.XP6qA_ZFw2x.

2. Ibid.

3. pilgrimplace.org

Chapter 6

Transformational Thinking

He said to him, "You shall love the Lord your God with all your heart, and with all your soul, and with all your mind." (Matthew 22:37)

The intellectual adventure has often been underrated among congregants and pastors. Many congregants look for entertaining rather than reflective sermons, and they would prefer to dwell on the surface, sound-bite level, of critical ethical issues instead of wrestling with the complexities of ecology, social justice, abortion, and physician-assisted death. Choked by the weeds of everyday ministry, the seeds of theological and biblical reflection planted and watered in seminary often fail to grow to their full potential in the lives and ministries of pastorals. Despite these realities, I have found that, given the opportunity, there is a critical mass of congregants who want to grow intellectually as well as spiritually and who want to explore the challenging issues of pluralism, truth, ethics, and scripture. Like the young Jesus at Temple, they want to grow in wisdom and stature, whether at five, thirty, or ninety-five.

For four decades, I have challenged my seminary students and newly ordained and commissioned pastors to claim the role of theologian of their congregations. I remind them that even if their former theology and bible professors are members of their congregation, they are the ones who rise to the pulpit Sunday after Sunday to share the good news of the gospel, interpret scriptural passages, and connect the wisdom of the Christian tradition with the maelstrom of critical ethical and personal issues of our time. In the course of a year, the average congregational pastor, whether solo or senior, may preach as many as 45–50 sermons, amounting to over 200 pages of writing, equivalent in length to most books published. As I tell my students, "you have no choice but to be a theologian. This is what your congregation needs, even if they don't always say so. Your calling is to be the best and most articulate theologian, with your gifts and the particular characteristics of your congregation." Every pastor's vocation involves seeking to live up to the words of II Timothy 2:15, inscribed on the childhood bible given to me at Community Baptist Church, King City, California, in 1961: "Do your best to present yourself to God as one approved by him, a worker who has no need to be ashamed, rightly explaining the word of truth."

Jesus championed a holistic theology, embracing body, mind, spirit, and relationships. The healer from Nazareth charged his followers to "love the Lord your God with all your heart, and with all your soul and with all your mind, and with all your strength" (Matthew 12:30). We are urged to love God with our minds. To me, this means that we become truth-seekers in our intellectual, political, and vocational lives. It means to provide theological comfort, but stick to the facts in a time of national crisis, such as the COVID-19 pandemic.[1] We scour the resources of faith, what Albert Outler described as the Wesleyan Quadrilateral of scripture, experience, tradition, and reason. We also listen for God's voice speaking through the creativity and conflict of literature, movies, science, and poetry. A dynamic faith must go beyond easy answers as we witness the events of the day, reported on NPR, PBS, CNN, MSNBC, FOX network news, or alternative stations such as Pacifica, and information on our Internet feeds. As Proverbs 8 recognizes, Divine Wisdom shouts to us on the street corners, inviting us to discern God's pathway in the hubbub of twenty-first-century social change, political incivility, and planetary threat.

As I grow older, I become convinced of the truth of Paul's counsel to the Christians at Rome:

> Do not be conformed to this world, but be transformed by the renewing of your minds, so that you may discern what is the will of God—what is good and acceptable and perfect. For by the grace given to me I say to everyone among you not to think of yourself more highly than you ought to think, but to think with sober judgment, each according to the measure of faith that God has assigned. (Romans 12:2–3)

Paul challenges us to be open to continuous intellectual and spiritual creative transformation. To follow God's way is to chart a path, different from the mores, values, and stereotypes of our culture. At any age, we are challenged to seek the truth, including truths about ourselves and our relationship with God, as essential to our ongoing spiritual and intellectual growth. While Paul's counsel applies to our knowledge of God and ourselves, his words are critical in our understanding of the aging process and our vocations in retirement. "Do not be conformed to this world" of ageism, superficiality, stereotypes, and limitation. Don't let the world of superficial age denial squeeze you into its mold, substituting apparent youthfulness for lifelong wisdom. Don't succumb to the hedonism of grandparents spending their children's inheritance on environmentally destructive baubles; live joyfully but plan your lifestyle to ensure wellbeing for generations you'll never see.

As I move toward retirement, sometime in the next few years, I am grateful beyond words for my intellectual acuity, opportunity to study with some of North America's if not the planet's leading theologians, collegiality with intellectually gifted peers, and the ability to study and write in the context of my pastoral, administrative, and teaching duties. I feel blessed that my current congregation supports my theological and spiritual adventures, reflected in weekly classes in scripture and theology and monthly seminar on mysticism at church and my seminary teaching at Wesley Theological Seminary in Washington DC. I can joyfully admit that my integration of the often siloed worlds of pulpit and classroom, pastoral care and study, and administration and writing has deepened not only my academic life but also my ministry as I have sought to embody what Etty Hillesum describes as a "thinking heart" in every aspect of my professional life. I am grateful to the generosity of my congregation and the Louisville Institute for providing new opportunities for intellectual exploration.

While I cannot predict the future, I am inspired by the generativity of my academic mentors John Cobb and David Griffin, who now in the nineties and eighties, respectively, still write and provide guidance in responding to global climate change and issues of ethics and public policy. It is my personal hope that long after I leave full-time ministry, I will continue to write and share my gifts as a teacher whether in a congregation, seminary, university or community college, or senior center.

Each pastor is called to explore their own gifts. Still, all pastors are also invited to nurture mind and spirit as well as body and relationships. Lifelong learning is necessary for those retired pastors who are committed to generativity, making a difference in their communities in terms of transforming the church, supporting the growth of the next generation, or confronting the injustices of our times. Our attention may move from the seminary library to the Internet and hardbound books to kindle and nook. Growing in wisdom and stature means following our gifts and interests to increase our own experience of life and be resources for change in our communities.

LOVING GOD WITH YOUR MIND

Studies suggest that intellectual activity not only deepens our understanding of the world but also it is a factor in overall well-being and healthy mental acuity. Like any other muscle, the mind flourishes when it is active and creative. We are at our best, whether as companions or citizens, when we go beyond the surface of life to discern the complexities and nuances of politics, culture, literature, and religion. While not everyone is a bibliophile or scholar like me, varieties of mental activity—even playing word games on your cell phone—energize and enliven our cells as well as our souls.

A former seminary student of mine, Diane admits that her mind is constantly going. Creative thoughts constantly come to her throughout the day, and often she chooses to act on them to improve her family life and community. "My gifts as a pastor-administrator are constantly being called upon in my retirement. Still, I don't have any ambition to stand out intellectually these days. God is calling me simply to be and enjoy each day as it comes." Although she shares her insights in ways appropriate for her status as a retired pastor, Diane no longer wants to be center stage as a congregational change agent.

An avid reader, now Diane receives her greatest joy from the time she and her husband spend reading out loud to one another before retiring for the night. When we talked, she revealed that they were currently reading *Amish Grace: How Forgiveness Transcended Tragedy*, recounting the Amish community's response to the Nickel Mines School tragedy.[2] Among their other adventures in couple's reading are texts by Wendell Berry, Richard Rohr, and Mary Oliver. "We talk about what we're reading, pondering together the theological, spiritual, and ethical questions raised. It binds us together as a couple." Diane has rediscovered the social dimension of study that inspired her in seminary. As a teacher-administrator prior to entering seminary, Diane appreciates the joy and synergy of learning with others, especially learning new things with her husband.

Reading is also one of the ties that binds Catherine and her husband. She notes that now that she is retired and "she has time to read." An extrovert, she found herself so caught up in the various tasks of ministry that, in her words, "I barely had time to do any study except for my sermon preparation and sadly that was usually last minute on Saturday night and Sunday morning. Now I have the leisure to let what I read soak in and change the way I look at the world."

While once she read on the fly, now she belongs to two book groups, one at the church and another with women friends in the community. She is especially grateful that her husband is a member of the couples' reading group at church. "Reading has become an important part of our relationship. We enjoy talking about the books we're reading, and this is way that we grow together in our relationship."

Well into their nineties, a clergy couple, one of whom was on the faculty at a New England seminary, spent every morning prior to their deaths joining worship and reading. After their morning prayers, they settled down to read a theological classic, often a text they had first encountered in seminary. One morning when I dropped by to serve communion, I found them reading Dietrich Bonhoeffer's *Cost of Discipleship*. Actively reading each morning until the last few months of their life together, in their quiet way, this clergy couple kept the flames of theological reflection alive, nurturing their minds despite the diminishment of age.

Suzanne is intentional in focusing on her intellectual growth.[3] Now that she is retired, she and her husband read the *Washington Post* each morning, circling articles that interest them. Her equally intellectually curious husband and she join daily in the news of the day, creating what she describes as their "newspaper club." Often on the road, Suzanne is a fan of audio books and subscribes to Kanopy, a video streaming service, obtained through her public library. Letting her curiosity run free, she and her husband explore other cultures and then plan their next journeys.

Suzanne and her husband Dan continue their intellectual quest by yearly visits to the Chautauqua Institution in Eastern New York. A week in Chautauqua is filled with lectures on various topics in current events, history, sociology, religion, concerts, and classes in literature and the arts. Prior to her retirement, Suzanne enrolled in Parker Palmer's "Soul of Aging" program to prepare her for retirement as well as to enable her to provide spiritual guidance to pastors and laypersons in search of zestful and meaningful responses to the realities of aging.

Peter, a retired western Massachusetts United Church of Christ pastor, was burned out when he retired.[4] He had been exhilarated by urban ministry, but the capital campaign in the last few years of his ministry wore him down. Initially, the movement from fast pace at church to no pace in retirement was a shock to his system. Peter recalls his daughter taking photographs of him during the first six months of his retirement. When she showed them to him, he admitted that "I looked like a wreck. I needed to find something to nourish my mind and spirit or I would go downhill fast." Peter had always enjoyed writing sermons and short articles for the church newsletter and local paper, so writing seemed like an obvious pathway out of his malaise. Like myself, Peter embarked on a daily writing regimen, combining creativity with writing for the well-being of others. In exploring his own lifetime choices through his daily writing, Peter was able to pen a text aimed at helping retired persons like himself make positive decisions. "Working on a book," Peter recalls, "pulled me back to where I wanted to be emotionally, intellectually, and spiritually." As a result of his writing on what he calls the "ten dimensions of retirement," Peter began giving seminars and ten-week courses related to his book at churches, senior centers, and retirement communities. "I have more invitations these days than I can respond to," he happily noted. Peter is currently working on a book of meditations and photos connecting the seasons of the calendar year and the beauty and wildness of nature with the seasons of the Christian year. He anticipates that this will keep him busy for quite a while in researching and writing, since he is endeavoring to address the spiritual possibilities of fifty-two Sundays![5]

After my father died, I discovered a vast corpus of poetry he had written during retirement. Although he described his poetry as "doggerel," unpretentious and simple, my father's poems reflected his encounters with God as he faced his life as a widower. In like fashion, Gordon began to pursue poetry in advance of his retirement. Known for his well-crafted, inspirational, and often prophetic sermons, Gordon Forbes, cited earlier, sought a different media for literary expression. Poetry focused his mind, and then let it run free, as he spent hours looking for the right word to describe the relational, natural, and political around him. Like Peter and my father, Gordon made writing, along with daily devotions with his wife, an essential part of each day. Retirement can be a jubilee of the mind in which we explore adventures of ideas, ranging from writing in the local newspaper to contemplating the cosmos.

PATHWAYS TO JUBILEE

I believe that God speaks to us in our cells and our souls. God's voice whispers to us in our thoughts, insights, inspirations, and questions. Whole person retirement involves using your intellectual gifts as fully as possible to discern God's vision for you and the world and to experience the joy of learning.

Books that Changed Your Life

A poster in the Lancaster School of Theology library pronounced, "I always imagined that heaven will be a kind of library." I endorse that sentiment. Books have played a central part in my spiritual and professional growth. I have grown in wisdom and stature through reading widely across religious, cultural, and theological lines. Research for books I'm writing has broadened and deepened my self-understanding and increased my empathy for others. In the course of writing this book, I consulted over fifty books, written by persons of a variety of gender, ethnic, sexual, political, and denominational perspectives. I have also explored the theological, philosophical, spiritual, sociological, literary, and medical dimensions of aging and retirement.

Although I was raised in a Bible-believing church, I left the faith as a teenager and was ambivalent about Christian faith even after I returned to church in college. I was wondered if my questions about the resurrection and deity of Christ might somehow disqualify me until I read Paul Tillich's *Dynamics of Faith*. Tillich saw doubt as an essential aspect of faith, a sign of the seriousness of a person's faith journey. We only doubt and question what is important to us. In my own life, I only wrestle with issues that are truly important to me. We can compare our intellectual questions with our care for our closest relations. I take questions about my marriage and the marriages of relatives and dear friends seriously. I don't give the same seriousness thought to other relationships, not because these relationships are unimportant, but because my intimate relationships are existential in nature. I ask questions about God, prayer, and survival after death because such issues are a matter of life and death for me and guideposts for my ethical and political involvement. Over the years, books continue to shape my spiritual life. As an avid reader, it is difficult for me to single out one particular book, but rather scores of books that have shaped my vision of the world, including Plato's dialogues, Alfred North Whitehead's *Adventures of Ideas* and *Process and Reality,* John Cobb's *Christ in a Pluralistic Age,* and the writings of Howard Thurman. My spirit has been nurtured and transformed by reading the works of Madeleine L'Engle, Mary Oliver, Annie Dillard, Walt Whitman, Rumi, and Ralph Waldo Emerson. Time after time, I come back to Jean-Pierre de Caussade's *Sacrament of the Present Moment, The Way of the Pilgrim* written by an anonymous Russian mystic, Brother Lawrence's *The Practice of the Presence of God*, and the wisdom of mystics such as Francis of Assisi, Julian of Norwich, Hildegard of Bingen, Mechtild of Magdeberg, and the Desert Mothers and Fathers and Celtic spiritual guides. I regularly teach new courses and revise courses at seminary and our church to keep up with theological, cultural, and spiritual changes as well as to support my own intellectual and spiritual growth.

As you reflect on your adventures in intellectual growth, I invite you to imaginatively explore your relationship with books. Visualize the books you read as a child. What books do you remember as most meaningful to you? Did you enjoy reading? What role did reading play in your intellectual development?

Repeat this same reflective exercise with focus on your youth and college years, young adulthood, midlife, and retirement.

Looking at your whole life, what books have been most pivotal in shaping your faith? Take time to revisit these books and consider their meaning for you now.

As you look toward the future, what role do you want reading and other intellectual activities (writing, learning online, journaling, classes) to play in your life? What new books and media are awaiting your explorations?

Conclude your spiritual practice by giving thanks for the books that shaped your personal and professional life along with those teachers who encouraged you to grow in wisdom and stature.

Growing Edges of the Mind

Loving God with your mind is not just an intellectual pursuit. It is a whole person adventure of the spirit, embracing our senses as well as our intellect. As Candace Pert noted in her *Molecules of Emotion,* brain-like receptors are present in our intestines, suggesting that the mind is nonlocally present throughout the body. The body is inspired and the mind is embodied. Accordingly, intellectual adventures involve learning new skills. A pastor friend of mine, who had never played an instrument, became part of a ukulele band. Another retired pastor took up the cello in his mid-sixties and now belongs to a local string ensemble. Travel enlarges the mind and broadens our perspective. As Jimmy Buffet notes, changes in latitudes lead to changes in attitudes. Travel host and writer Rick Steves speaks of travel in terms of expanding our ethical and spiritual horizons. We become more cosmopolitan as we interact with people of different of nationalities and ethnicities. At sixty-seven and sixty-five, respectively, my wife and I were part of a leadership team for a pilgrimage to Assisi. We walked the paths of St. Francis, imbibing Franciscan spirituality along with Italian wine! We recently returned from our first sojourn to Nova Scotia to enjoy the Cape Breton Celtic festivals, to meet retired Canadian pastors, and to speak at the Atlantic School of Theology. We have trips to Scotland, England, France, and a voyage down the Danube, and the USA Southwest on our agenda over the next few years.

Holistic spirituality includes our hands and heart as well as our head. Steven, a retired pastor from Michigan, describes the transformative experience of volunteering to help build Puerto Rican houses in the aftermath of Hurricane Maria. "I had never spent much time on carpentry and helping rebuild homes gave me new muscles as well as new skills." Instead of just writing a check to Habitat for Humanity, Steven now participates in house raisings in his local community. "I say prayers and give devotions, and I also put up siding and carry materials. I also research on the causes of poverty and ways our nation can address the needs of its most vulnerable people."

Looking at your life, what are your adventurous growing edges, joining mind, body, and spirit? As Sufi mystic Rumi says, there are a hundred ways to kneel and kiss the ground. There are also hundreds of ways to grow intellectually and experientially. To plum the depths of your artistic and intellectual growing edges, take an afternoon to ponder your gifts, talents, and inner creative urges. These can be artistic, horticultural, musical, theatrical, or literary. Imagine yourself living into new possibilities. What is your heart's and mind's passion? What might it look like to begin a new personal adventure? What first steps would launch you on this creative pilgrimage? Take time to give thanks for God's creativity flowing through you as you take live out the new possibilities for intellectual and personal growth.

Living Affirmatively

As I noted earlier, affirmations are essential to spiritual growth and positive aging. Paul counsels us not to let the world squeeze us into its mold. Many retired persons struggle with age-related stereotypes. These stereotypes limit our creativity, agility, and adventurousness. In contrast, biblical spirituality, lived out in the maelstrom of conflict and mortality, proclaims that God actively moves in our lives, providing us with unexpected possibilities and the energy and guidance to achieve them. God has plans for us, at every age, for "your welfare and not harm, and for a future with hope" (Jeremiah 29:11). The earliest Christian communities were challenged to trust God's expansive vision for their lives, congruent with Jesus' own promise that he came that we "have life and have it abundantly" (John 10:10).

> Now to him who by the power at work within us is able to accomplish abundantly far more than all we can ask or imagine, to him be glory in the church and in Christ Jesus to all generations, forever and ever. (Ephesians 3:20)

Affirmative faith challenges us to let go of our self-imposed limitations and embrace God's possibilities. I use a variety of affirmations, one of which has shaped my life as a writer. Before going to bed, I often briefly review what I plan to write the next morning. After looking over the notes, I affirm that "God will give me insight, inspiration and creativity for my writing tomorrow morning." When the new day begins, sometime between 4:30 a.m. and 5:30 a.m., I take a half an hour for prayerful contemplation as my coffee brews, grab a cup of coffee, sit down in my arts and crafts recliner chair, and begin to write. Typically, the words flow as if I have working all night on the morning's writing assignment. Perhaps, I have. My evening affirmation awakens my unconscious resources—the Holy Spirit's "sighs too deep for words"—as the foundation for my predawn writing.

Practicing affirmative prayer begins with a prayerful Examen, regarding your attitudes toward aging as a prelude to renewing your mind through spiritual affirmations. After a time of silence, take time to explore your images of aging in general and your own personal aging process. What images do you have? How would you judge these images? Are they accurate or inaccurate? What limits do these images and the self-talk that goes with them place on your life?

As a second step, consider healthy and realistic self-talk that counters these images. Our self-talk or affirmative faith needs to be concrete as well as positive. Affirmations do not deny concrete situations, but challenge limitations we place on ourselves in these situations and conditions. They claim a deeper realism, grounded in God's ever-present companionship and inspiration. My use of spiritual affirmations is grounded in Paul's words to the Philippians:

> Whatever is true, whatever is honorable, whatever is just, whatever is pure, whatever is pleasing, whatever is commendable, if there is any excellence and if there is anything worthy of praise, think about these things. (Philippians 4:8)

In the following paragraphs, I will share affirmations that have been help-ful to me and persons with whom I have shared spiritual guidance. Because I believe that affirmations are essential for intellectual growth, I am elaborating on an earlier spiritual exercise related to affirmative faith. Affirmations take many forms and foci. For example, someone who is overweight might use the following affirmations:

I eat healthy foods that promote physical well-being.
My body is healthy and beautiful.

Someone who is dealing with feelings of scarcity and lack might choose the following affirmation:

I have all the time, talent, and treasure to serve God, experience
    fulfillment, and bring healing to the world.

As we face anxieties in terms of aging, and our concerns for our diminish-ment, we might consider the affirmations such as:

Nothing can separate me from the love of God.
God is with me in the darkest valley.

And then substitute a word that addresses your current condition in the affir-mations such as:

Aging cannot separate me from the love of God.
 Illness cannot separate me from the love of God.

The biblical tradition provides a variety of life-transforming affirmations, which can transform the way we look at the world:

I can do all things with Christ who strengthens me.
I have the mind of Christ.
I am God's companion in healing the world.
My God will satisfy all my needs through God's abundance.
I am the light of the world. God's light shines in me.
Whether I live or die, I am in God's hands.

Grounded in God's graceful presence, affirmations expand my vision, promote well-being, and fill us with hope and courage to face the challenges of life.

Read with a Child or Adult

Good ministry is grounded in study and intellectual curiosity. Virtually every minister I interviewed in this study is a reader and regular visitor to their local public library. Recognizing our interest in reading, we can use our gifts of reading to help others experience more abundant life.

I am the "homework grandpa" in our family. I read with my two grand-sons four or five times a week, just as my father read with me and I read with their father. We have worked together on a couple unpublished short books. In addition, I volunteer as a reading coach on a weekly basis with second and third graders at their school, a practice I hope to continue in the years ahead. Reading with adults has been found to be essential to a child's love of learning and intellectual growth. In this spirit, consider volunteering to be a mentor, tutor, or coach in an area of personal interest of expertise, whether it be reading, history, science, or mathematics. With the coming of the Coronavirus, my professional flexibility has allowed my wife and I to "homeschool" our grandchildren now that the schools have been closed.

Many elders also appreciate finding someone who will read with them. They may be dealing with sight impairment or simply want the company. You may find another senior adult who loves to read books of shared interest. You both will grow relationally, imaginatively, and intellectually.

Prayers for the Pathway. Loving God, awaken me to beauty and love. Open my senses to your presence in my life and my identity as your beloved child. Help me to move from darkness to light, and scarcity to abundance. Let me trust you to supply my deepest needs. Let the mind of Christ dwell in me, shaping my vision and actions. In Christ's name. Amen.

NOTES

1. Bruce Epperly, *Faith in a Time of Pandemic* (Gonzales, FL: Energion Publications, 2020).

2. Donald Kraybill, Steven Nolt, and David Weaver-Zercher, *Amish Grace: How Forgiveness Transcended Tragedy* (San Francisco, CA: Jossey-Bass, 2010).

3. Her actual name.

4. Real name.

5. Peter B. Ives, *What Is Your Life? Discovering What Matters Before It is Too Late* (Northampton, MA: Paradise Copies, 2015).

Chapter 7

Living in the Spirit

Then the LORD appeared to Abram, and said, "To your offspring I will give this land." So he built there an altar to the LORD, who had appeared to him. From there he moved on to the hill country on the east of Bethel, and pitched his tent, with Bethel on the west and Ai on the east; and there he built an altar to the LORD and invoked the name of the LORD. (Genesis 12:1–12)

The story is told of the biblical adventurer, Jacob, who one evening, weary from his travels, lay down with stone for a pillow. In the course of the night, Jacob had an amazing dream in which he saw angels ascending from earth to heaven and then back to earth. Overwhelmed by his encounter with the Holy One, Jacob stammered, "Surely the LORD is in this place—and I did not know it!" And he was afraid, and said, "How awesome is this place! This is none other than the house of God, and this is the gate of heaven" (Genesis 28:16–17). In response to his encounter with the Holy One, Jacob named the place, Beth-El, the gateway to heaven.

While pastors seldom have mystical experiences as dramatic as Jacob's, virtually every pastor I have met has experienced the call of God, luring them into spiritual leadership. In telling their call stories, retired pastors talk about the moment they could no longer put off going to seminary. "It was as if God had been calling me all my life, and finally I knew I had to give in. When I said 'yes,' I had a deep sense of peace that I was finally on the pathway that had prepared for me from birth," so recounts Susan, a second-career United Methodist pastor. Others, like my father, felt the call from childhood that came to fruition with the GI-bill, college, and seminary after World War II. My aunt Beulah recalled hearing my father preaching to the chickens at age five and thinking that "someday he'll be a minister." In the spirit of Isaiah at the Temple, Drew heard God's voice at summer youth camp in Ohio.

Around the campfire, the camp director asked, "Who is willing to follow Jesus?" Drew remembers, "Deep inside, I knew this was the time. I raised my hand, came forward to the center of the circle, and dedicated my life to Christ. I knew God had a plan for me, and I wanted to serve him." Ten years later, Drew entered seminary and spent nearly forty years pastoring American Baptist congregations. My wife Kate made her commitment to "serve God" around a campfire at Camp Christian in Ohio. She initially thought it was to serve God as a teacher, since there were few models for women in ministry at the time. But, following graduation from college, she worked for the Stanford University YMCA, where she observed Diana Kenney, now retired in Pilgrim Place, California, and discovered that now the call was to follow Jesus as a pastor.

My own sense of call began to surface in college. I returned to church, after venturing into the Summer of Love, studying Buddhism and Hinduism, and pursuing mystical experiences. In search of a spiritual practice, I learned Transcendental Meditation in October 1970, and started attending the college church, Grace Baptist, the next week. I began to study theology and saw myself as a religion professor. As I delved into the Christian mystical tradition, I felt a persistent, but quiet movement, to join ministry with the academic life. I wanted to give something back to the progressive church that nurtured me. I wanted to share a positive Christian message that was deeply spiritual and theologically open.

Ministers are, in the words of theologian and biblical scholar Marcus Borg, spirit persons who have encountered the Holy and are called to enable others to experience the divine in their own lives. Ministers are the spiritual children of the magi, shaman, wise woman and wise man, medicine person, and sage. Even we find ourselves choked by the thorns of congregational ministry, we experience beneath the maelstrom of ministry the reality that "deep calls to deep" (Psalm 42:7), the voice of God moving through our lives, persistently calling us back to our vocation.

Pastors are spiritual and sacramental persons whose task is to share the gospel of God's graceful and life-changing presence in our lives. In the spirit of the prophets, pastors may also be social activists but their picketing is joined with prayer. Marching against injustice to borderland children, violence against the LGBTQ or unfair police practices toward persons of color, pastors may experience the spirit moving in protest, as Rabbi Abraham Joshua Heschel recalls from marching with Martin Luther King, "I felt my legs were praying."

Jacob's encounter with the Holy One reminds me of the Celtic vision of "thin places," spots where the veil between heaven and earth is lifted and earth becomes transparent to the divine. Jacob discovers in the course of his life that Beth-El is everywhere. Every place we go is a gateway to heaven.

Every encounter can become a thin place in which we are touched by God, opening our senses to the holiness in our midst. This is surely the meaning of divine omnipresence. Wherever we go, whether in times of elation or depths of despair, God is with us, gently—and sometimes dramatically—calling us to wake up to God's loving presence.

We live in a God-filled world. As William Blake avers, "If the doors of perception were cleansed, we would see everything as it is—infinite." Each moment is sacramental, calling us to respond to God in every situation, as Jean-Pierre Caussade counsels. That is the heart of the spiritual adventure!

PRACTICING HOLY ADVENTURE

I believe that, when we are aware of the holiness of life, our lives become a holy adventure with God as our guide, challenger, and companion. Our ultimate calling is to claim our role as God's companions in healing the world, one action at a time, one moment at a time, and one day at a time. The spiritual journey involves our growing awareness that "God is in this place," wherever that place happens to be, health or illness, joy or sorrow, prosperity or adversity. Whether we live or die, we are God's beloved and dwell in the palm of God's loving arms.

God often comes to us unbidden. We are all mystics, all open to God's "sighs too deep for words" as they well up from our unconscious, awakening us to a sense of divine wisdom and guidance. We also encounter God through apparently chance, but often providential encounters. Still, when we open our senses—cleanse the doors of perception—through spiritual practices, such as worship, prayer, meditation, mindfulness, sacrifice, and service, God comes alive for us, whether in the pulpit or eating dinner with our life partner.

The Sufi poet and mystic Rumi asserts that there are a hundred ways to kneel and kiss the ground. There are many paths to God, depending on our personality type, family, and religion of origin, social location and context, life experiences, daily responsibilities, and previous encounters with the Holy. These paths to the divine typically involve the dynamic interplay of vision, promise, and practice.

Broadly speaking, our theological vision is the spoken or unspoken lens through which we experience the world. Our vision of reality reflects our images of God, the divine—human relationship, the role of the earth and embodiment in spiritual growth, understanding of human possibility, and our understanding of the joyful and painful realities of life. Our theological vision provides a sense of what is important and what is optional in our personal and political lives and inspires us to behave in ways that embody our highest values.

Our vision is grounded in God's promise that those who call upon God will be saved, that is, find wholeness. God promises that we can experience our deepest visions of reality as pathways to abundant life and God consciousness. Jesus tells us that he is the vine, the life-transforming energy of the universe, and that when we connect with him, letting his energy of love flow through us, we will bear much fruit. God wants us to have abundant life and is constantly providing for our deepest needs. We simply need to say "yes" to God's grace and let God's promises enlighten, energize, and empower.

Practices are the pathways to healing and fulfillment, to unity, congruence, or companionship, enabling us to live out presence in our lives. Our practices are the ways we "ask, search, and knock" in our quest for God. Our practices are our response to God's call, our placing ourselves in a place of grace that enables us to experience from our limited vantage point the length and depth of God's presence and vision for our lives.

When she sees me meditating or giving myself a Reiki treatment, my wife Kate occasionally jokes, "Your auditioning for sainthood, aren't you?" And, to some extent, she is right, if the quest for sainthood involves opening to God's light and letting that light flow through you to bless and heal the world. Since I first learned Transcendental Meditation in 1970, contemplative prayer has been central to my life, whether with my original TM, or Centering Prayer and Breath prayer. Typically my day begins in a monastic style: I awaken between 4:30 a.m. and 5:30 a.m., repeat the Psalmist's affirmation, "This is the day that God has made and I will rejoice and be glad in it," and then take twenty to thirty minutes for meditative prayer, study for an hour, before going out for a solitary prayer walk on Craigville and Covell's beaches and through the picturesque neighborhood of Craigville. I return to study and write, before taking another half an hour for meditation before turning to church-related activities. Sometime during the day, I will lie down and give myself a Reiki treatment. Reiki healing touch is a Japanese healing practice, aimed at enlivening and channeling God's healing energy (chi) to promote personal and spiritual well-being. I first learned Reiki healing touch, a cousin of acupuncture, therapeutic touch, Tai Chi, and Qi Gong, in the mid-1980s. In the early 1990s, I received the master-teacher level of Reiki and have taught hundreds of people Reiki healing touch over the years. For me, Reiki is prayer with your hands and is one way we can meditate the healing power of Jesus, the true light that shines in and through all of us. In addition to Reiki, meditation, and walking prayer, I regularly pause throughout my day, assessing my spiritual state and then breathing deeply God's presence in my life.[1]

In the spirit of Philippians 4, I also use affirmative prayers throughout the day, including affirmations such as:

I give Christ to and receive Christ from everyone I meet.
I bless everyone I meet.
Every breath I take is a prayer.
God is supplying all my needs.
I can do all things through Christ who strengthens me.

When I feel anxious or at risk, I bring myself back to God's presence by reciting Psalm 23 or by repeating Paul's promise: Nothing can separate me from the love of God.

In my daily spoken prayers, I focus on giving thanks for the wonders of my life, asking for guiding, praying for my congregation, and interceding, sometimes in words, other times in images, for persons in need or who have requested my prayers. Like one of my spiritual mentors Dag Hammarskjold, I believe thanksgiving for all that has been and for the privileges I have experienced awakens me to the great "yes" of God's vision for the future.

While I recognize that I may be unusual in my use of several practices on a daily basis and regular commitment to spiritual disciplines, these practices have shaped my ministry, provided consolation in times of pain, empowered me to face conflict, inspired greater creativity, and strengthened me in the quest for justice. They have enlarged my world and helped me find peace amid the storms of life. For me, prayer and meditation are the great connectors, inspiring me to move from self-interest to world loyalty.

RETIREMENT AS AN INVITATION TO SPIRITUAL ADVENTURE

Just as chronic and life-transforming illness do not immediately call forth spiritual resources, retirement does not, in and of itself, inspire greater commitment to spiritual practices. As theologians and spirit persons in their congregations, pastors should be cultivating spiritual practices throughout their ministries. From the beginning of their seminary education, they should undergird the arts of ministry with contemplative prayer, healing practices, and prophetic prayerfulness. While seminary students often come to seminary with a Godward orientation, they regularly complain that their spirituality is given short shrift as they confront the challenges of theology, biblical studies, church history, church administration, and pastoral care classes. Seminarians often find few models of integrative spirituality among the ministers with whom they train. During a clergy career, spiritual practices often become optional as a result of the demands of congregational administration, outreach, pastoral care, and sermon preparation, even though all of these can be defined as spiritual in nature. Ironically, many pastors confess that now that they are retired from full-time ministry, and they have time to cultivate their spiritual lives and experience the life-changing significance of worship for the first time.

There are numerous ways to nurture spiritual depth in retirement. Donald states that he does not devote a specific time of day to prayer and meditation. For him, spirituality is ambient. It is a matter of attention and orientation, what some call mindfulness. According to Donald, "Throughout the day, as I go from one activity to another, I try to see every encounter as a way of meeting Christ. In my work with persons experiencing substance use disorder and homelessness, I try to follow Mother Teresa's counsel to see Christ disguised behind the challenges they face. I may not be disciplined enough for regular prayer and meditation times. In fact, I've failed at daily centering prayer. Still, I want my whole life to be a prayer, not just a few dedicated moments." Although he struggles with a regular discipline, Donald follows the spirit of Brother Lawrence in practicing the presence of God moment by moment.

For some retired pastors, worship is central to their spiritual journeys. A Cape Cod clergy couple in their nineties nurtured their faith by daily prayer. Although they were no longer able to attend church regularly, they read together the Office of Morning Prayer from the Book of Common Prayer. Their prayer time bound them to the faith of the church universal and reminded them that God was with them, despite the infirmities they experienced. Their daily prayers were visible signs of their relationship with communion of saints, which was their comfort in the present and hope the future. A high point of my own pastoral ministry was to celebrate communion with this faithful couple. I often arrived at their home right after their morning prayers. There was a profound sense of peace on their faces, which filled their woodland home. Usually quite progressive liturgically, I honored their sense of tradition and always read a version of the Book of Common Prayer eucharistic service with them. Now deceased, it is my hope that this couple is now singing "Alleluia" with one another in God's realm of Shalom, where there is no sunrise or sunset or beginning or end.

Worship is central to the spiritual life of Karen, a retired Disciples of Christ minister, who, by her own admission, was "so busy with the mechanics of worship that she had trouble worshipping" during her thirty years of congregational and university ministry. These days Karen surprises her friends when she tells them that most Sundays she worships at two churches. Each Sunday, she and her husband attend the early service of an affluent, multi-staff suburban United Church of Christ congregation, where "my soul is fed by the high-quality worship and preaching." She finds it exhilarating to worship with others and always "comes out feeling like I have so much left to give to this world." Following the first service, she often drives to a small Disciples of Christ church five miles away. "The worship and preaching are heart-felt, though not as polished or professional. But what I love is the diversity of the membership. People of all races and economic situations attend this church." Karen rejoices at the opportunity to worship with two very different congregations: "I love it. It reorients my week. I am learning to be part of a community as a parishioner not a pastor. I enjoy receiving so I can give in the week ahead." Extroverted my nature, Karen experiences the Holy most fully in community, "where I can pray and praise with people around me, each of us doing the best we can to be faithful in a challenging world."

Linda describes her current spiritual practices as "fairly traditional," with their focus on stewardship and worship. She has discovered that generosity has given her a new perspective on life, widening her spirit and sense of concern for others. Now that she and her husband have greater financial largesse, they have chosen to contribute to certain charities and political movements beyond the church as well as their local congregation. Still, in examining her stewardship, Linda confesses, "I still feel like I want to give more. The need is so great in our church and in the world. We are becoming more intentional about our giving, and that has help us expand our giving. We're getting closer to giving what we want to be giving." Recently, Linda and her husband made a sizable donation to the private religious school where she served as headmaster before attending seminary. She sees this gift as generative in nature. "I am giving back to a community that nurtured my faith at a difficult time. I want this gift to help support this school's mission for generations to come." Linda has discovered that stewardship can be a form of prayer, as authentic as worship or contemplation.

Linda's greatest spiritual renewal comes from her participation in the Episcopal church, located in her small upstate New York community. "I enjoy the church from the pew side nowadays. I loved leading worship, but now I can receive the spiritual nurture I need." She is grateful that the rector has invited her to lead retreats and teach classes at church. "Preparing for these programs enriches me spiritually," she notes. After spending many years focusing on her own healing and spiritual growth, Linda is claiming as a retired pastor her vocation as God's partner in the healing of others. "God is saying to me, 'You've done all this work on yourself, you've got to use it in the healing of others.'"

Although she does not meditate regularly these days, Linda, like David, admits that her spirituality is incarnational and domestic in nature and relates to every aspect of her life. "God is in everything I do, including my marriage, volunteering with hospice, small town social involvements, and grandparenting. I'm living out what it means to pray without ceasing in my domestic life and relationships. It feels authentic, and right for me to see my whole life as spiritual, and not just the 'religious' aspects."

My friend of nearly three decades Suzanne describes her spirituality in terms of the "three C's"—community, connection, and curiosity.[2] Community gives us an opportunity to give and receive, in the spirit of one of Suzanne's favorite poems, Marge Piercy, "To Be of Use." In community, Suzanne notes, "we share in creation as creators along with God." In connection, "we allow ourselves to be shaped and shape others in relationships." Curiosity is a spiritual virtue, grounded in the varieties of human experience and the immensity of the universe. Curiosity joins "mind and spirit, as we seek to learn about other peoples' cultures, religions, and spiritualities." There is always more to know about God and the world, and the horizons are always receding, and curiosity opens the door to ongoing adventures.

Regularly meeting with a spiritual director has been at the heart of Suzanne's spiritual journey for over twenty years. She consulted her spiritual director as she considered retirement and now that she is retired regular meetings with her spiritual director give direction and support her ongoing spiritual growth. Suzanne notes that her spiritual director constantly asks her, "What are you learning from this experience?" This has helped Suzanne discern her own personal pathway toward jubilee living.

Many pastors, like me, carry decades-long spiritual practices into retirement. Sharon has been practicing yoga and sitting meditation with her attorney husband for over two decades. She has led yoga retreats and meditation classes at her congregations as a way of deepening persons' faith as Christians. "Yoga and meditation have deepened my Christian experience. I hear the still, small voice of God more clearly as a result of my joining Hindu and Buddhist spirituality with the teachings of Jesus." She takes seriously Vietnamese Buddhist monk Thich Naht Hanh's "engaged Buddhism," joining of mindfulness with social concern, and calls her own practice "engaged Christianity." She notes,

> now that I am retired, I have more time for yoga and meditation. I go on retreats at a local Buddhist meditation center and I teach yoga and centering prayer at a local Episcopal church. Retirement has given me more time for silence, including more time to take my silence out into the world, engaging injustice with a calm and caring spirit. My spiritual practices help me stay centered in the political world, preventing me from getting caught up in the polarizing and name calling of persons whose viewpoints I oppose. I can see them as God's children and still challenge the injustice and planetary destruction they perpetrate.

Today's retired pastors are surrounded by a cloud of witnesses whose spirituality undergirds their lives and inspires their social activism and daily commitments to family and friends. I mentioned earlier the witness of Dorothy

Day, one of my models for generative spirituality. Although as a Roman Catholic, she was never ordained, the example of social activist, crusader for the marginalized, and founding mother of the Catholic worker movement in North America, Dorothy Day helps me to face my own anxieties about health limitations as I grow older. In her seventies, sidelined by health issues and no longer able to run the Catholic Worker paper or travel to protest injustice, she confessed that "my job now is prayer."[3] In that short affirmation, Day models a spirituality for retired pastors and spouses who no longer can leave their homes and participate as agents of compassion and change. My Cape Cod congregants embodied the same hopeful spirituality, praying with one another and for the world each morning as part of their daily spiritual disciplines. In our infirmity, we can still pray, feeling God's presence, and interceding on behalf of the world in all its tragic beauty.

Walter Wink once noted that the future belongs to the intercessors. What would happen if retired pastors and their spouses along with millions of persons, confined to their homes, assisted living, or nursing care facilities took an hour a day for prayer, praying a simple prayer such as the Jesus Prayer, "Lord have mercy upon me, a sinner" as a mantra for our own lives and the country or visualizing God's light permeating places of fear and pain? What if we all prayed—as well as acted—to respond to the injustices of our time. Such prayers of affirmation would take us beyond the cramped worlds of infirmity and connect us with the wellsprings of Shalom, flowing through our lives and the world. Confined to a wheelchair or homebound, we still could take our role as God's companions in healing the earth. Such prayers would in the poetry of Harry Emerson Fosdick's "God of Grace and God of Glory":

Save us from weak resignation
to the evils we deplore;
let the search for thy salvation
be our glory evermore.
Grant us wisdom, grant us courage,
serving thee whom we adore,
serving thee whom we adore.

I believe that by our prayers for the planet, our world be transformed and come nearer to embodying Jesus' prayer that God's realm come "on earth as it is in heaven."

PATHWAYS TO JUBILEE

Ordination is a lifelong calling, and so is our vocation as spirit persons. God is present in our lives regardless of the quality of our awareness. God is, as the apostle Paul preaches to Athenian intellectual community, the reality "in whom we live and move and have our being" (Acts 17:28). "God is in this place and now we know it" is the heart of the spiritual journey. The truth that there are a hundred ways to kneel and kiss the ground invites us to be spiritually creative, exploring a variety of ways to experience God's multidimensional presence in the world.

THE MOVEMENTS OF PRAYER

The author Anne Lamott describes prayer as a process embracing "wow," "thanks," and "help," to which I would add "inspire." In this spirit, consider the following movements in your prayerful practices:

"Wow," the sense of radical amazement, to quote Rabbi Abraham Heschel, at the wonders of the universe and your own existence. You might repeat a chant I learned at the Shalem Institute for Spiritual Formation, "I thank you God for the wonder of my being" and then follow with "I thank you God for the wonder of all being."

"Thanks" for the providential presence of God in your life and the world. God's providence has guided us through all the changes of life, sustaining, protecting, and guiding. Take time to "count your blessings" for God's great faithfulness in all the seasons of life.

"Help" as the recognition of our dependence on God's presence to guide our pathways. We are all, as the spiritual pleads, "standin' in the need of prayer." We need guidance and sustenance from a power and wisdom greater than our own. We need God every hour and every moment of our lives.

Finally, awakening to God's inspiration. Ask God to "inspire" you in the next steps of your spiritual journey and your involvement as God's companion in healing the world. Following Isaiah's experience in the Jerusalem Temple, we discover that inspiration is grounded in the interplay of God's call "whom shall I send" and our willingness to respond, "here I am, send me." Invite God to use our time, talent, and treasure for the well-being of our congregations, communities, and the planet.

Opening to Silence

Psychiatrist and spiritual guide Gerald May counsels spiritual seekers to "pause, notice, open, yield, and respond" to God's presence in our lives. Spiritual growth is about the interplay of self-awareness and God awareness. In fact, in knowing God we know ourselves, and in knowing ourselves we come to know God. In the storms of retirement, we experience God in the "still, small voice," the "sheer silence," of divine guidance.

To open to silence, we first pause to open to the movements of God in the "sighs too deep for words." God is whispering in our lives and when we listen, we experience divine power, presence, and guidance. We also notice the deeper realities of life, flowing in and through us, giving us energy and direction. What we experience in stillness may surprise and, at times, overwhelm us, and we need to yield to God's amazing and awesome energy of love, the energy of the big bang that enlivens cells and souls. The experience of yielding inspires us, as it does with spoken prayers, to respond in service to humankind and the planet.

Whereas one of the movements of prayer may involve our calling out to God, another aspect involves holy listening. We listen to our lives, as Frederick Buechner counsels, and then with Parker Palmer, let our lives speak!

Seeing Deeply, Acting Boldly

A bench at the Kirkridge Retreat Center in Bangor, Pennsylvania, challenges us to "picket and pray." Spirituality involves integrating the inner and outer journeys, care for the soul, and care for the planet.

Thomas Merton ventured forth one day from silence of the Trappist Monastery at Gethsemani, Kentucky to walk the city streets of Louisville. As he walked the busy streets of Louisville, Merton's eyes were opened and saw Christ in all the passersby:

> At the corner of Fourth and Walnut, in the center of the shopping district, I was suddenly overwhelmed with the realization that I loved all those people, that they were mine and I was theirs, that we could not be alien to one another even though we were total strangers.
>
> It was like waking from a dream of separateness . . . The whole illusion of separate holy existence is a dream.[4]

In that moment of spiritual transformation, Merton realized that the most enlightened and most benighted persons reveal God's presence. Merton discovered that true spirituality connects because life is connected. In Christ, there is no "other," for God meets us in every human face. Our calling in full-time ministry and retirement is to see God in every face and then work to create the circumstances in which everyone can experience life in its abundance.

Seeing Christ in others challenges us to being Christ in relationship to others. As Christ's emissaries in every season of life, channeling Christ's mission in our time, we must embrace a spirituality of compassion that awakens us to awareness and action to the plight of children separated from their parents on the U.S. borders, single and economically disadvantaged mothers considering abortion, persons of color experiencing discrimination by the legal system, and the well-being of our planet. Seeing God in the nonhuman as well as human world awakens us to a planetary ethic that looks generations ahead rather than to the next stockholders' report. Our prayers may lead us to picket, phone, protest, and politic. Our meditations may take us to town hall, the school board, or planning board hearing. Practicing the presence of God involves far more than finding God in the kitchen or sanctuary, which may mean finding God in the House of Representatives or pounding the pavement for candidates which reflect an inclusive, compassionate vision.

A Prayer for the Pathway. Loving and Embracing God, open my heart to your presence. Help me to pause and notice the wonder of my life and this good earth, and in my awe, let me experience the joy and pain of all creation. Let me attentive to where your footsteps lead me. Let me see your face in every face, and from that vision, claim my place as your companion in healing the world. In Jesus' Name. Amen

NOTES

1. Bruce Epperly, *The Energy of Love: Reiki and Christian Healing* (Gonzales, FL: Energion Publications, 2017) and Bruce Epperly and Katherine Epperly, *Reiki Healing Touch and the Way of Jesus* (Kelowna, BC: Northstone Books, 2005). Also, Bruce Epperly, *Healing Marks: Healing and Spirituality in Mark's Gospel* (Gonzales, FL: Energion Publications, 2012) and *God's Touch: Faith, Wholeness, and the Healing Miracles of Jesus* (Louisville: Westminster/John Knox, 2001).

2. Real name.

3. Dorothy Day, *Selected Writings: Little by Little* (Maryknoll, NY: Orbis Books, 2005), xl.

4. Thomas Merton, *Thomas Merton: Essential Writings* (Maryknoll, NY: Orbis, 2000), 90.

Chapter 8

Changing Relationships

Beloved, let us love one another, because love is from God; everyone who loves is born of God and knows God. Whoever does not love does not know God, for God is love. (I John 4:7–8)

The philosopher Alfred North Whitehead asserted that the whole world conspires to create a moment of experience. Every person emerges from an intricate fabric of relatedness. It takes a village to raise a child, nurture a relationship, and support a pastor. Healthy relationships are grounded in our affirmation of the South African concept of *ubuntu*, "I am because of you."

Ministry is relational in nature. In course of a week, most pastors touch scores of lives, shaping and being shaped by their encounters with pilgrims, patients, persons in need, and students. Even those of us who enjoy the solitude of study and contemplation know that our solitary ruminations find their fulfillment in our public ministries of preaching, teaching, pastoral care, spiritual guidance, and protest. We are blessed to bless others.

Healthy ministry involves an interplay of giving and receiving, not just in congregational life, but in our relationships with friends, family, and professional colleagues. When pastors retire, many of these relationships are professionally terminated. Pastoral boundaries mean that we must let go of relationships that may have spanned generations. Letting go is often difficult, especially in relationship to those congregants who have depended on our pastoral care or with whom we have uniquely intimate and positive relationships. I am already doing some anticipatory grief as I ponder leaving a congregation I greatly love sometime in the next five years. As one pastor noted, "breaking up is hard to do," especially when we are bonded with our congregations. Grief attends any significant professional and personal loss, and this even applies to pastors who maintain clear and healthy boundaries. Leaving a congregation affects spouses and partners as well as pastors. Husbands, wives, and partners may have developed significant friendships over the years in men's and women's groups, soft ball teams and golf foursomes, choirs, social groups, and outreach programs. Even though they are not retiring, and have independent relationships within the congregations, they must also let go of certain close relationships to give space for the next pastor and her or his family. Retirement is especially difficult for single pastors, widows, and widowers, pastoring in rural congregations, where it is often the case that their primary relationships are within the congregation, as the result of few opportunities to cultivate relationships with friends outside the congregation. They are faced with looking a new home in a community, often with few or no relationships in place.

As scripture says, it is not good for a person to be alone. We need intimates with whom we can share our hearts and minds, whether spouses and partners, close friends, children, and grandchildren. As I look toward my own retirement, I feel both blessed and challenged. My wife and I have a close personal and professional relationship, spanning over forty years. My son, his wife, and our two grandchildren live a mile away in a neighboring Cape Cod. My immediate relational life is rich, with my family and professional life. Should my son and his wife choose to move, it is likely we will relocate as well. Nevertheless, I don't have many close friends outside my family, and few close friends on the Cape. I realize that I need to cultivate a handful of personal friends and begin to do so before retiring. Although I love solitude, I know that my intellectual and spiritual life is fed by teaching and conversation. At this point of my life, like other pastors considering retirement, I need to become intentional in cultivating relationships to enrich and sustain, as well as to serve, in the years ahead. While the relational paths are many for pastors, they share the spirit of connection, healing, partnership, and commitment in all the seasons of life.

ON THE OUTSIDE LOOKING IN

While many retired clergy can maintain denominational relationships following retirement, many of the pastors with whom I corresponded no longer felt connected with the denominations where they had served for decades. Steven notes, "For a number of years, I was active in diocesan activities and was regularly asked to serve on committees and attend events. When I retired, the phone stopped ringing. I still wanted to be involved but it seemed like my name was crossed off the list."

Annie added, "At first I felt alienated from my peers. But then I got over it. I discovered that if I wanted to be active in the denomination, it was up to me. I reached out to the bishop and let her know I was available for anything that might match my gifts. Soon my phone was ringing again. She asked me to be on a mission committee and to reach out to newly ordained ministers in the area. I feel like I'm connected once more, giving back what I received from experienced pastors three decades ago."

Diane, an Upper Midwest United Church of Christ pastor, feels ambivalent about her place in the church following retirement. Speaking for many of the pastors I interviewed, Diane reflected on her experience as a recently retired pastor:

> Where do I fit in? Pastors are centers of attention and we like it, and now we are on the sidelines? What do I have to share? Will anyone pay attention? Too often we define ourselves by our role, and that's built into the nature of the job. It's whole person and touches every aspect of our lives . . . The transition was hard for me, and a lot of my colleagues, when you're pastor, you get a lot of attention. When you're retired—you're nothing.

Diane eventually found her place as an environmental educator and advocate, working in the secular world as well as a church consultant.

Although there is a tendency among denominational leaders and committees to overlook retired clergy, for a variety of reasons, including the perception that retired clergy need to disengage from the daily rounds of ministerial service, those pastors who reach out to their denominations leadership generally find new ways to serve: on committees, supply preaching, transitional interims, sabbatical interims, and mentoring. Our willingness to serve the larger denomination or support a local ministry is often welcome when we take the initiative. Our gifts and experience often respond to local or regional needs.

Recognizing the realities of isolation in retirement, a group of pastors on Cape Cod where I live formed a Community of Practice, sponsored by the Massachusetts Conference of the United Church of Christ. This gathering of pastors meets monthly throughout the year to discuss theological and ministerial issues, reflect on the aging process and retirement, and support each other's journeys. Most of them have settled at the same Cape Cod church, where they, with the affirmation of the pastor, do occasional preaching, pastoral care, and singing in the choir. Other pastors have created informal groups or regular coffee breaks to sustain one another and grow spiritually by sharing in a book group or simply enjoying each other's company. During my tenure at Lancaster Theological Seminary, I was able to create several retired pastors' groups to ease the transition from congregational leadership to retirement. Whether it is in making new friends or staying active in ministerial activities, it is important for pastors to be creative in responding to the novelty of retirement. We need to take initiative, once we have a good sense of our hopes for retirement, in growing relationships with colleagues, service programs, or new friends.

HEALING RELATIONSHIPS

The Christian vision of human existence recognizes that we are all on a journey, incomplete, and in need of one another. Paul notes that in the body of Christ, the many parts support one another and those aspects of the body that receive the most public attention are undergirded by the parts that are considered mundane and unpretentious. Within the interdependence of life, we rejoice in each other's achievements and mourn each other's losses. Within the healthiest relationships, we also accept each other's fallibilities and forgive one another's imperfections. The process of forgiveness and healing requires patience and is the project of a lifetime. Yet, in coming to terms with each other's uniqueness, with the wholeness of our companions in life, we discover the holiness embedded in every committed relationship. We will experience the face of God in the expressions of our loved ones.

Laura sees cultivating healthy relationships as a spiritual discipline. She asserts that she is "now that in a position time wise and financially to strengthen relationships with her family." As a single parent of four children with minimal financial and personal support, life was not easy for her children or herself. She often had to scrimp and save and was often away from home for long hours in her role as a teacher and educational administrator. In retirement, this second-career pastor has the time to spend time with her four children, two of whom have grandchildren. She notes, "I am part of my grandchildren's lives and am getting to know my own children as adults and peers." A recently remarried widow, Laura also sees deepening her relationship with her husband as a spiritual issue. "We're learning to be the couple we're supposed to be. Marriage, children, and grandchildren definitely reflect God's call in my life, and now I want to be faithful in nurturing these loving relationships."

Laura sees healing at the heart of her relationships, most especially with her dysfunctional family of origin. "I was grateful for the opportunity to become closer to my sister before she died. My brother and I are also growing together after having lived separate lives for many years." She is seeking the same healing in her own family, recognizing that although she gave her children all the love she could during their childhoods, the absence of their father and her long hours at work have left wounds and resentments. Laura believes that "God is calling me to be part of a healing process in my family of origin and with my own children." Her own commitment to personal healing is enabling her to be a healing companion with her family.

Commitment is the word that best describes Sandra's relationship with her mother. After early retirement due to disabilities that made full-time ministry impossible, Sandra moved in with her homebound ninety-two-year-old mother. "I needed a place to live as I began the next season of life and my mother needed my support." A single second-career Disciples of Christ pastor, Sandra left her congregation in Iowa to return to Pittsburgh to be with her mother. "Mom is struggling with diabetes and mobility problems, and has trouble sleeping at night, so—even with the home health care aid—I spend most of my day at home and often sit with her till she falls asleep in the early hours of the morning." Sandra recognizes that she has sacrificed the free-wheeling retirement advertised in the media. She also recognizes that her love for her mother more than makes up for any sacrifice she is currently making. "My mom loved and raised three children, now it's my turn to give back, and though some wouldn't want to be in my shoes, I am grateful for the opportunity to these years with Mom, nurturing and loving her, and enabling to live at home. Sometimes I think I could have made other decisions, but this is the path I've chosen and it's not really a sacrifice."

Having recovered her own personal well-being and ensured good home care for her mother, Sandra is now broadening her horizons and venturing forth to become active in a local congregation and begin to explore part-time employment as a way of employing her own pastoral gifts.

Another disciple of Christ pastor, Bill, recognizes that retirement is not what he and his wife expected. When I spoke with him at his home in Phoenix, Arizona, Bill and his sisters were preparing for a trip to Alaska. He is also pondering where he and his wife will be living in retirement. Shortly after he retired, his wife was diagnosed with Alzheimer's disease in her late sixties. She is happy and mobile, and still go on trips with the support of family members, but their life will never be what they had initially planned. Bill has three children, all living on the Eastern seaboard, and he wants to locate near the grandchildren as well as to have support for his wife should he falter. To the surprise of many, Bill notes that "Alzheimer's has enriched me. I have learned what patience means." Bill asserts that "I trust that the Sacred is present in all things. It is a new adventure for me and my wife. Not one I had planned. It's not the silly childish golden years that we are promised, but it's something more profound, living out the vows my wife and I made forty years ago, now when it really counts."

Like the magi who visited the newborn Jesus, Bill is "going home by another way." Having recently celebrated their forty-eighth anniversary, Bill shared that "I'm trusting the Holy One that somehow through all of this, we will be just fine in this life and the next." As Bill and I talked, we both were reminded of the joy that comes from a lifelong commitment in all the seasons of life and how the vows we made when we were young and in love now challenge us to become persons worthy of the love we been given. A lifelong relationship is not always easy, but through the sacrifices we make and the healing we seek, we surely grow in wisdom and stature and favor with God and humankind. Bill and I celebrated the joy of a long-term committed relationship as we meditated on the vows he made almost a half-century before. "Now I am living out what we vowed so long ago, and I'm grateful that I am with her

For better, for worse.
For richer, for poorer.
In sickness and health.
To love and to cherish
As long as we both shall live."

ADVENTUROUS RELATIONSHIPS

Suzanne met a new friend on a Viking ship tour of the Rhine with her husband.[1] When Suzanne initially saw this woman across the room at a shipboard party, she thought, "There was something special about her. She's going to be my new friend." As they got to know one another, they discovered that they had a great deal in common including the joy of reading.

Although they live across the country in Maryland and California, respectively, they make an appointment to talk about books on a monthly basis. They call their club, "Books for Two." Currently, Suzanne noted, they are reading a book I recommended, Mary Pipher's book on the spirituality of aging, *Women Rowing North*.

After she purchased a home near her children and grandchildren, June discerned a deep need for a lasting and intimate relationship. As a widowed pastor, she had few opportunities to date. While she felt content with her life, June wanted to share her joy with a life companion. She took a risk and registered for an over fifties online dating service, prayerfully considered what she wanted in a husband. She had several "first dates" until she finally found Walter, a man whose values, lifestyle, personality, and plans for retirement mirrored her own. They took it slow, getting to know one another as friends as well as lovers. After a year, they became engaged and now are "living the dream" of small-town life, with three generations of family within twenty minutes. "I'm glad I took a chance on love again. I prayed a lot before registering on the dating site, and then prayed as our relationship grew. God had God's hand in my marriage, and I am grateful that our relationships matter to the Creator of the Universe."

Diane notes that many pastors move after they retire from congregational or institutional ministry. Her counsel is "to get to know the community. Meet people and get to know life outside the church—and there is life outside the church! We need to remind ourselves that there are communities and tasks to do outside the church, whether in volunteering to tutor, getting involved in local politics, or committing yourself to political activism for human rights, justice for immigrants, building a house for Habitat for Humanity, or coaching a sports team."

Travel guide Rick Steves describes travel as a political act which changes our perspectives, enlarges our appreciation for pluralism, and deepens our empathy for persons of different cultures, faiths, and value systems. In the spirit of singer-songwriter Jimmy Buffet, changes in latitudes can lead to changes in attitudes. Many retired clergy can attest to life-changing perspectives that emerge from the going beyond the familiar to the novelty of foreign lands and unfamiliar regions of our own country. Bob and Ruth, retired United Church of Christ pastors, belong to a travel club that specializes in low-cost tours. Unencumbered by children or grandchildren, Ruth rejoices that Bob and Ruth can "get up and go whenever the opportunity arises. In the past three years, we've been to Greece, Turkey, Italy, Sweden and Norway, Scotland and Ireland, Vietnam, and Australia. We didn't take time to travel with the demands of ministry and our tendency to be workaholics. But, now, with few responsibilities other than occasional supply preaching, we're off to see the world."

Bob adds, "It's been eye-opening. We try to get to know the people and learn what's important to them. We've realized that we are so different and so alike. We've lost our sense of American exceptionalism and parochial small-town ministry values and are becoming citizens of the world."

"Nowadays," Ruth laments, "I find it hard to imagine that some of the folks in our Midwest churches have never left the state they were born in, much less traveled to the state capitol. No wonder they're so easily seduced political perspectives that trade on fear of people of other nationalities and races. I only wished we'd traveled more in our ministerial years. We might have helped our congregants see the world more broadly and less fearfully."

LETTING GO AND COMING BACK

Clergy retirement typically means a complete, or significant, break from one's final congregational position. Good boundaries suggest that a retired pastor finds a new place to worship and seldom returns to their former congregation, either to attend services or perform weddings or memorial services, without the express affirmation of their successor. Although this is generally good advice, there are always exceptions. Some pastors return to their former congregations as active ordained/congregants, enjoying relationships with former congregants, while affirming the gifts and authority of their successors.

At the conclusion of their ministries, many congregations and pastors
share in a service of celebration and letting go. Even the best of pastor–parish
relationships is imperfect. Despite our love for our congregants, we know as
pastors that there have been times when we have let them down, responded
meekly when we should have acted decisively, cared too much or cared too
little, or missed pastoral opportunities. Pastor and parish alike have missed
opportunities for faithful and innovative ministry. While there may be times
in which the "Love Story" maxim "love is never having to say you're sorry"
is appropriate, healthy relationships involve the recognition of fallibility,
limitation, conflict, and carelessness. Recognizing the need to forgive and be
forgiven, even in the best of ministries, enables pastor and congregation alike
to move forward in ministry, giving thanks for all that has been, and saying
"yes" to God's future for us.

A service for the "Ending of an Authorized Ministry" may be especially
meaningful when this ending coincides with a pastor's retirement. Several
pastors noted that members from previous congregations were in attendance,
offering their gratitude and support. These pastors also noted that their
expressions of gratitude, forgiveness, and letting go related to their whole
career and not just their final congregational call. They recited:

I ask forgiveness for the mistakes I have made.
I am grateful for the ways my ministry was accepted.
As I leave, I carry with me all that I have learned here.

In response, the gathered congregation responded:

We receive your thankfulness, offer forgiveness,
and accept that you now have to minister elsewhere.
We express your gratitude for your time among us.
We ask your forgiveness for our mistakes.
Your influence on our faith and faithfulness will not
leave us at your departure.[2]

In hearing these words, several pastors commented that they experienced
a cloud of witnesses of congregants, colleagues, and communities present
with them, despite the differences in space and time. While our ministries
are always geographically and chronologically located, a lifetime of pastoral
ministry embraces every pastoral encounter and the impact of our ministries
on people we have never met or will ever meet.

Although it is common practice for pastors to leave their congregations
permanently upon retirement, on occasion when a pastor returns, after an
appropriate absence, both congregation and pastor are blessed. Henry retired

from a large Disciples of Christ congregation in the Midwest. In his fifteen-year ministry, Henry and his wife Elaine had purchased a home and put down roots in a midsize town, equidistant from their two children. When he retired, Henry and Elaine chose to spend the next three years traveling, developing new friendships, and spending time with their children and grandchildren. Henry did two short-term interim ministries, filling three-month gaps before the arrival of the settled minister. At the end of three years, Henry and Elaine met with the settled pastor, expressed their desire to return to the congregation they had served and people they cherished, and agreed on appropriate boundaries for their participation in the congregation. The new senior pastor was mature, talented, and confident in his gifts. He did not feel threatened by the presence of a former pastor in the congregation. Still, the senior pastor and Henry met with the church's leadership to measure their response to Henry and Elaine's return. Everyone agreed to welcome Henry and Elaine back, recognizing that although they would be active members, any pastoral responsibilities would be at the senior pastor's discretion. Henry spoke with emotion and gratitude as he reflected on "my new beginning at my former church. Most of the time I just attend. Elaine is back in the choir and the women's group, and I have helped the pastor out with the capital campaign and community outreach. Other than that, we simply enjoy worshipping God in a community we love and under the leadership of a talented and inspirational pastor."

Still, quite healthy, Henry and Elaine know that someday the pastoral roles will be reversed. Their pastor will companion them in sickness, grief, aging, and death. "It's good," Henry confesses, "to be at a church I love and, frankly, the only one in the area, I would want to attend. I am grateful for a welcoming pastor, confident enough to make room for us. My goal is to support her and the other staff and be a helpful part of the body of Christ."

Mark took a similar path, leaving a church he had pastored for thirty-one years, and then coming back at a new pastor's invitation. Mark retired early at sixty-two, having pastored with excellence, but feeling the stresses and strains of ministry in multicultural, metropolitan congregation. Mark admits, "When I retired, we never dreamed that we'd be coming back. We didn't want to get in the way of a new pastor." Mark took seriously the counsel of his thirty-year-old son, who noted, "Dad, you're giving up a job, but Mom's giving up everything, her best friends, her volunteer work with the homeless, and her church. You owe it to her to go to a church that blesses her." They found a congregation of another denomination where they both enjoyed the preaching, worship, and fellowship. When the newly settled pastor called asking them to come back to the congregation Mark had pastored when he retired, they did not say "yes" until they spoke with the Regional Minister and several clergy colleagues. At that point, Mark and his wife Dawn "were able to go back. My wife got involved in the homeless program she had initiated years before. It was good to be home again." While Mark kept a low profile, after a few years, he was asked to become an "elder," a spiritual leader of the congregation, once again with his pastor's affirmation. When a newly settled pastor came to the church, Mark gave him the option of having him leave the church. The new pastor responded, "It would be an honor for me to be your pastor." Mark and Henry have flourished in their former congregations as a result of several key factors: (1) confident and competent pastoral leadership, able to affirm the presence of a former pastor without anxiety or defensiveness; (2) a clear sense of boundaries and strong support of the settled pastor by the returning retired pastor; and (3) a willingness of former congregants to redefine their former pastor as a friend and fellow congregant rather than pastor.

After several years of pastoring a congregation thirty miles from her home church, Suzanne decided to return to the church that "sent her off into ministry." Her husband had remained involved in the congregation, rotating between the church he had attended for two decades and the congregation Suzanne pastored. Before deciding to return, Suzanne had a long talk with the current pastor, alerting her that "she didn't want to do a thing for a year." Suzanne appreciates the intellectual depth and spiritual maturity of the current pastor and finds herself fed by her sermons and worship leadership. Now, after three years of attending, Suzanne regularly does pastoral care when her pastor is away on holiday or at conferences. When I spoke with Suzanne, she informed me that she is looking forward to "preaching again at my home church. The pastor will be away on retreat, and she asked me to preach on 'community engagement' in her absence. I'm looking forward to preaching. It is important for me to give something back to the church that nurtured me, not as pastor but as an active congregant, worshipping among friends."

Since returning, she has partnered with a retired Presbyterian minister who also attends the church to encourage greater community involvement by the congregation. In this role, she sees herself as an adjunct and supporter to the pastor.

Suzanne affirms curiosity as an important spiritual and relational virtue. This has motivated her to seek out relationships with younger people. Now almost seventy, she regularly reaches out to couples in their thirties and forties, as well as their young children. "I am constantly interested in learning new things and getting out of my relational comfort zone. I want to see the world from perspectives different than my own. Life is about growth and one of the best ways to grow is to engage in relationships with persons with very different experiences, whether cultural, racial, or demographic."

Yes, growth is at the heart of healthy relationships in retirement. Relationships change and we need to be willing to explore new possibilities with our loved ones as well as widen the circle of our friendships. Augustine once asserted that "if you think you know it, it isn't God." The same applies to our relationships. We must let our life partners surprise us and be willing to surprise ourselves by new ways of responding to them, letting go of past habits so we can grow into new possibilities.

PATHWAYS TO JUBILEE

Healthy relationships can be the tipping point between life and death, and success and failure. Even the most introverted and monastic clergy are nurtured by relationships, including spiritual guides, colleagues, partners, and the literary and historical traditions of faith, theology, and spirituality. No person is an island in an interdependent universe. Retired clergy and clergy preparing for retirement often reflect on the quality of their relationships and ways that they experience greater relational meaning and fulfillment. Relationships change when we leave full-time ministry. No longer at the heart of congregational life, where will we satisfy our needs for connection, affirmation, and challenge?

A Relational Examen

In this spiritual practice, we will focus on the quality of our relationships as essential to spiritual and personal growth. Our relationships can be catalysts for spiritual growth and creativity. They can nurture our hearts as well as our minds. A relational Examen involves the following steps:

1. After a time of stillness, give thanks for the wondrous world that sustains you and your family in body, mind, spirit, and relationships. Affirm the generous interdependence of life, grounded in God's graceful providence and embodied in nurturing relationships.
2. Review your current relational situation, reflecting on the quality and quantity of your relationships. With whom are you most intimate? With whom do you experience joy and meaning? How much time do you spend cultivating healthy and meaningful relationships?
3. Notice your overall attitudes toward your current relationships. In what ways might you deepen your relationships? Do your relationships deepen your relationship with God?
4. Identify one aspect of your relational life as an inspiration to prayer and, possibly, creative transformation.
5. Look toward the future with gratitude and resolve to move forward toward deeper and more meaningful relationships in the present and the future.

If certain aspects of your relational life need deepening or healing, ask for God's guidance for next steps in transforming these relationships.

New Possibilities in Marriage and Friendship

The concrete world is the womb of possibility. Our current situation relationally is an invitation to imaginative thinking. In the spirit of the point–counterpoint of Frederick Buechner and Parker Palmer, "listen to your life" and then "let your life speak." Looking at your current close relationships, what aspects of these relationships gives you the greatest joy? Given your sense of joy, contentment, and fulfillment, in what ways can you deepen these relationships? For example, in areas such as communication, intellectual synergy, joint projects or avocations (travel, volunteer work, domestic activities), intimacy and sexuality, nurture and support. Take some time over the next several days to visualize this hoped-for growth occurring and enjoying renewal and revitalization in your relationships.

If you are able, take the first steps to embodying new possibilities in a close relationship. Explore new ways to interact and take risks with new behaviors. Ask for God's guidance one step at a time.

If you discover that certain relationships need healing, ask for God's guidance in first steps in the healing process. Where do you need to practice forgiveness? Affirmation? Letting go? Be open to the guidance you receive, knowing that you are only responsible for your own healing process and your desire to heal relationships with others.

Praying Relationships

Retirement awakens us to new sides of ourselves and those we love. In long-standing relationships, we often take our companions for granted. We see persons in certain frames of reference and certain habitual responses and overlook their uniqueness. We no longer notice or identify with their feelings. Healthy relationships involve constant care to maintain a high level of empathy and consideration. Prayer connects us with the deeper experiences of those we love, enabling us to grow in empathy to see them as God's beloved children.

In this spiritual practice, take some time for contemplative visualization. In your imagination, see those whom you love with deep empathy, feeling the unity of your experience and theirs. Then, visualize them permeated and surrounded by God's light, beloved, and beautiful.

Throughout the day, pause to notice and then open to the experience of your loved ones. Look deeply into them, experiencing the holy light shining in and through them. Respond with acts of love and compassion, reaching out in care and support.

A Prayer for the Pathway: Loving God, to whom all hearts are open and every experience treasured, wake me up to the beauty of those around me. Help me see them as you do, as your beloved children, and treat them with great reverence and love, seeking their well-being as well as my own. In Christ's Name. Amen.

NOTES

1. Real name.
2. Book of Worship, *United Church of Christ* (New York: United Church Office for Church Life and Leadership, 1986), 256.

Chapter 9

Companioning with God

If I am not for myself, who will be for me?
If I am not for others, what am I?
And if not now, when? (Rabbi Hillel)

Knowing I would be writing on the theme of pastoral retirement, a friend of mine posted a humorous saying on my Facebook page, "pastors don't retire, they just go out to pastor." There is a good deal of truth in her message. All the pastors with whom I spoke affirmed their ministerial identity. Even those who were infirmed or taking a break from congregational involvement still claimed the spirit of their ordination vows. They saw themselves, in the words of Carter Heywood's frontier text on women in ministry, as a "priest forever." In holistic ministry, you cannot separate the person from their profession. Our character, ethics, spiritual commitments, and relationships matter in ministry. Although we all fall short at times, the calling of a pastor is to be a spirit person, a little Christ, an icon for holiness and transformation, a mediator of grace, and a companion in God's quest to heal the world.

The ordination questions of the Episcopal church capture a pastor's lifetime and whole-person commitment to serve God in all the seasons of life, regardless of their ministerial status:

Will you be diligent in the reading and study of the Holy Scriptures, and in seeking the knowledge of such things as may make you a stronger and more able minister of Christ? Will you endeavor so to minister the Word of God and the sacraments of the New Covenant, that the reconciling love of Christ may be known and received?

Will you undertake to be a faithful pastor to all whom you are called to serve, laboring together with them and with your fellow ministers to build up the family of God?

Will you do your best to pattern your life [and that of your family, or household, or community] in accordance with the teachings of Christ, so that you may be a wholesome example to your people?

Will you persevere in prayer, both in public and in private, asking God's grace, both for yourself and for others, offering all your labors to God, through the mediation of Jesus Christ, and in the sanctification of the Holy Spirit?

On the day of your retirement, you may let go of your professional duties as a pastor or chaplain, but you don't let go of your vocation to bring healing, justice, beauty, and salvation to the world. The Energy of Love and Creative Wisdom of God that propelled us into ministry continues after we have packed up our studies, put away our home communion sets, turned in our keys, and placed our robes and stoles in the closet. Despite professional changes, "we just go out to pastor."

God's call is intimate and universal. We are all called to a priesthood of believers, giving and receiving grace in our relationships and seeking to live a sacramental life. The universal call in always concrete, addressing us in terms of our gifts, life situation, religious communities, and unique graces for service. God's plenary call is also seasonal, contextual, and chronological. What we worked for in the first half of life we may need to jettison, and in the next half of life to be faithful to God's dream for our lives. Each moment, encounter, and season of life bring new possibilities to embody God's vision of Shalom and wholeness. Surely, this is at the heart of Therese of Lisieux's counsel to do ordinary things with great love, recapitulated by her spiritual follower Mother (Saint) Teresa of Calcutta, "do something beautiful for God."

Our vocation involves the dynamic interplay of our gifts and experiences and the needs of those around us, and this vocation is shifting moment by moment and season by season. It is my profound belief that retirement is an invitation to creative transformation. No longer hemmed in by congregational expectations, denominational politics, and our own need to please, we can stretch our spiritual wings and fly. We can more fully live out Luke's image of young Jesus growing in wisdom and stature and favor with God and humankind (Luke 2:52).

HEALING THE WORLD ONE ENCOUNTER AT A TIME

There is a saying from the Jewish mystical tradition, "the world is saved one person at time." The whole cannot be healed without the healing of the parts, and—in the spirit of Jesus' parable—the ninety-nine cannot find completeness without the return of the one lost sheep. Once again, consider first-century Jewish sage Rabbi Hillel's description of interplay of self-affirmation and service, central to the spirit of this book:

If I am not for myself, who will be for me?
If I am only for myself, what am I?
And if not now, when?

We find wholeness in loving our neighbors, those persons who are placed in our lives, with same care as we love ourselves. Each moment is a moment of healing and salvation, an opportunity to join the moral arc of the universe, perhaps, serving as a tipping point in bringing wholeness to the persons around you. Each moment is sacramental on the spiritual journey. According to Jean-Pierre de Caussade, "God still speaks today as he spoke to our forefathers in days gone by" revealing God's vision "in all things through faith."[1] Awakened to God's presence, "each moment imposes a virtuous obligation on us which committed souls faithfully obey. For God inspires with a desire to learn one moment what, in the next, will uphold them in the practice of virtue."[2]

De Caussade's wisdom has guided me throughout my pastoral, professional, and personal life, inspiring me to see divine providence in ordinary domestic tasks and everyday relationships as well as the more grandiose tasks of accompanying people in crisis, leading worship, and responding to the maelstrom of political and social issues in our time. It has become central to my understanding of the pathway of Jubilee during retirement. When we do ordinary things with loving care, the world is transformed regardless of the scope of our activity. In my late sixties, I see my vocation as multidimensional, with a major focus involving my two grade-school grandsons. Our daily encounters at soccer matches, reading together, driving to sports practice, going to the library, or simply "chilling out," help them discover their gives in each sacramental moment. I know that they will remain at the heart of my vocational life after I retire and help them navigate the waters of preadolescence and adolescence in an increasingly complex world. Aspiring to be a sagely elder, I share my wisdom with them, and perhaps, most important of all, share the gift of time and attention, of letting go of everything else to be with them in the Holy Here and Now. My grandparenting has invited me to care for other people's children, not just in our children's faith formation program at church, but also through tutoring in my grandchildren's classes. I plan to share my gifts in retirement in continuing adult faith formation and occasional seminary, community college, and senior center teach. I also plan to share my reading interest and writing skills with elementary and high-school students and local library enrichment programs.

Sometimes one act of hospitality opens the world to us. At a morning prayer gathering at Craigville Conference Center, a mile from our church, a retired pastor, now living in the Southwest, recalled being part of his Episcopal congregation's outreach to undocumented pilgrims on the U.S. borderlands. A mother brought her one-year-old child to him. She had been breastfeeding, but with the stress and uncertainty, her breast milk could no longer be counted on to nourish her young daughter. My friend mixed a little cereal with water and began to feed this little child. The child went after this simple meal as if it was manna from heaven, leaving both pastor and mother in tears. "Something small as cereal on a spoon can change a child's life. It changed mine." My friend discovered that the world is saved not just one person at a time but one act of kindness at a time. "That little girl was Christ to me, and now I know that as I do to the least of these, to this little child, I am serving Christ." Each person has a vocation, each season of life is vocational, and each moment is a call from God to "follow me."

Small acts, done with love, can change the world. After my Baptist pastor father's debilitating stroke, I discovered that in his retirement years he compiled a prayer list, wrote birthday cards, and made phone calls and visits to shut-ins from his church. The store clerks all knew him by name, citing "Mr. Epperly always had a good word to say. He asked about my family, comforted me when I was grieving, and simply cared, without need for any return on my part. I never knew he was a minister." No longer in active ministry or ever inclined toward social activism, my Dad still was a pastor, with his parish being the supermarket and shut-ins from church, healing the world one act at a time, and carrying forth his ministry without recognition or accolade; just being someone who cared, which was his calling for over forty years as a pastor.

As she prepared for retirement, Laura discerned that God was calling her to a unique ministry with persons facing death. I talked with this Pacific Southwest Unitarian Universalist pastor as she was recovering from shoulder surgery and preparing to embark on a regimen of physical therapy. She was looking forward to returning to her vocation as a therapeutic musician at a local hospice. Laura noted, as do many retired pastors, "You don't cease to be a minister upon retirement. Today, my ministry is music with persons facing death. I am a singer, and I sing favorites, traditional religious music, or improvise to provide companionship, comfort and palliative care, or to accompany persons in the dying process. Being a therapeutic musician is about being in the present moment, sharing in the experiences with another, and being of spiritual assistance."

Laura is clear that a therapeutic musician is not a performer but a spiritual companion. In many ways, she is performing the ancient vocation of psychopomp, accompanying souls in their journey from this world to the next. "I play and pray and do a ministry that helps people face their own mortality with a sense of peace and hope." Laura noted that her volunteer work at hospice integrates giving and receiving. She brings peace to others, and in the process she gains wisdom in facing her own aging and mortality.

Sandra retired from congregational ministry in 2015. Initially she dreamed of becoming a master gardener but discovered that she needed human inter- actions to feel fulfilled. In the course of her vocational investigations, she was invited to be a paid chaplain at the local hospice. Although it was an attractive possibility, Sarah realized that she prized her freedom. "I wanted to work with hospice but I didn't want to ask for vacation time or work pre- scribed hours. I wanted to spend my time giving back to the community and doing volunteer work best suited my life situation." Sandra volunteers at the local hospice, co-leading two grief groups with a bereavement counselor. She described the last session she led: "When the group's members arrived, I sent them out into the garden, inviting them to breathe deeply and enjoy the beauty of the environment. I invited them to think of hope and hopelessness and then talk about it." Although she considers herself a "minister incognito," wearing her professional status lightly, she is occasionally called upon to help family members plan memorial services and funerals. Recently remarried after being a widow for over a decade, Sandra sees her work as doing small things with great love. While she recognizes the importance of working in the political sphere, Sandra knows that her calling is to be God's companion, silently shar- ing in the healing of the world one loving act at a time.

Now retired after three decades of hospital, nursing home, and settled and interim ministries in Disciples of Christ and Presbyterian churches, Ellen believes that ministry is lifelong. "God puts people in our path and if we're open we can be both teachers and learners." An artist as well as preacher, Ellen spends much of her time teaching at a senior center associated with a major mid-western university. "I need to keep my creative juices going and this happens best when I help others be creative. After retiring, I took on-line courses with the Center for Journal Therapy, and now I use the techniques I learned to help my students, many of whom are older than me, to unlock their own creativity."[3] Journal therapy, according to Ellen, "unlocks our creativity, helps us learn about ourselves, and supports our healing process."

Ellen has also learned that her own pain can become a gift to others. Several years ago, Ellen's youngest daughter died of a rare cancer. Although she still grieves her daughter's death, Ellen has found a one-to-one mission in providing space for parents who have also lost children. "They know I understand. I have been in their shoes and still am. People come to me with their pain and loss and I'm a listening ear, who accepts how they feel because I've been there, too." Like Ellen, I believe that God is at work in our joy and pain. Although God does not choose our suffering and pain, still "in all things God works for good." Persons who create space for wounded people, "wounded healers" themselves, share in God's aim at healing and wholeness on person at a time.

SERVING IN UNEXPECTED PLACES

By anyone's calculation, Alice was a ministerial success. In her last congregational call, she led a church of oblivion to an average attendance of over 200 each Sunday, guided the congregation to welcome the LGBTQ community, and spearheaded programs to reach out to the working-class neighborhood. But, after fifteen years, the time had come to leave. "I had fulfilled my pastoral dream for this church. I could stick around a few more years and solidify our achievements. But I needed a change and so did they." In the months following her retirement, Alice prayed for new directions in her life and discovered a yearning for something quite different. "I wanted to be a regular congregant and I felt led to worship with the African American community." Alice gave feet to her prayers. One Saturday night, she scanned the Internet and came upon an inner city congregation. In her own words,

God guided my steps to go to a Baptist church in an economically struggling neighborhood ten miles from home. When I showed up, I was the only white person there, and when I sat in the back pew everyone stared at me as if to say, "What's that white woman doing here?"

Their stares turned to welcome, and after she was introduced, the pastor called her "Sister Pastor" and asked her to say a prayer at the conclusion of the two-hour service.

A week later over coffee, the congregation's pastor asserted "God sent you to me. I have been praying for God to send someone to help revitalize this church. Do you know anything about church revitalization?" When he heard about her pastoral experience, he asked, "Would you do series on church revitalization?" Alice responded with a resounding "yes." A few weeks later, the pastor introduced her to the congregation as "our new Associate Pastor." Alice serves without compensation, preaching, sharing in worship, and providing guidance in the congregation's revitalization process. Raised in a liturgical denomination, Alice quips, "I'm getting more Baptist all the time. This is my church. I will be buried here."

Karyn's retirement journey has taken her to theological seminaries in Liberia and Myanmar.[4] She enrolled in seminary after retiring from the police force with the rank of captain. After completing her M.Div. and Ph.D., Karyn served as an interim pastor in the metropolitan New York area for five years before retiring from congregational ministry. A liberation theologian by training, she felt God call her to teach theology in the developing, or what she prefers to call "the majority world." Karyn noted that as a result of finances and family situation, "I could do what very few liberation theologians are able to do—teach in the majority world."

For the past four years, Karyn has rotated three-month teaching assignments between Liberia and Myanmar. She feels called to present "an alternative to the fundamentalist perspective, sharing theological concepts of which the majority of her students were previously unaware." Her teaching is shaped, in part, by the work of Paolo Friere, author of the transformative text, *The Pedagogy of the Oppressed.* According to Friere, education is a grassroots process of dynamic co-creation in which teacher and student are partners in shaping the learning environment, thus empowering students to respond creatively to unjust social structures. Education transforms both the student and the world. While Karyn believes that God has called her to be a "volunteer" theological professor in the majority world, "the task of teaching in nations decimated by violence and civil war is challenging physically and emotionally." Although she lives in a seminary apartment during her overseas assignments, Karyn noted that "life in Myanmar and Liberia is filled with hardships that you don't experience in the United States." She feels great joy when she sees her students "thinking critically and exploring ideas that really matter" rather than blindly adopting fundamentalist theologies.

THE POLITICS OF RETIREMENT

Many pastors discover that their concern for social action matures in retirement. No longer burdened by church politics and the need to tamp down their political opinions to relate to politically diverse congregations, they make commitments to challenge powers and principalities, the forces of destruction, in the social and political order. They embody a saying, etched on a bench at Kirkridge Retreat and Conference Center in Bangor, Pennsylvania, "Picket and Pray."

Discouraged over the election of Donald Trump as president of the United States, Julia went with a dozen friends to march in Washington. Like Abraham Joshua Heschel, she felt like her legs were praying and that she needed to do more than march, she needed to act. A person of deep prayer, she asked God, "What role should I have in the Trump years?" The response came through a community need within her hardscrabble, rust belt community. "Work for justice. Help mobilize people to protect our rights and challenge the racism and fear of strangers in our community." Julia began to use her preaching and teaching skills to lead seminars in community organizing and activism, motivated by the words of Harry Emerson Fosdick's hymn, quoted earlier in this text:

Lo! The hosts of evil 'round us
Scorn Thy Christ, assail His ways
From the fears that long have bound us
Free our hearts to faith and praise
Grant us wisdom, grant us courage
For the living of these days . . .
Save us from weak resignation,
To the evils we deplore.
Let the search for Thy salvation,
Be our glory evermore.
Grant us wisdom, grant us courage,
Serving Thee whom we adore.

Julia affirms, "I've always been an activist, crusading for the LGBTQ community, farm workers and woman's rights. No longer tethered to a church, I can speak truth to power without concern for the consequences. I've always taken risks, but now I don't need to worry about how my politics affect the church."

Julia is often seen at rallies and protests and governmental offices in her variously colored clergy shirts and collars. She has worked on the borderlands, welcoming pilgrims from Central America, ensuring that they receive food, shelter, and legal aid. She shows up at Planned Parenthood, advocating for women's reproductive health and constantly challenges her representatives to challenge the current administration's "destructive environmental deregulations," believing that "we are at a tipping point. Will we choose life or death for future generations? Will we sell out the earth for short-term profits?" With John Wesley, Julia has discovered that her parish is the world, and that she must confront her nation's leaders when they succumb to what she believes is racism, xenophobia, sexism, homophobia, and environmental destruction. "I cannot as a Christian stand idly by, powerless while our leaders choose death. I must ask and then challenge when their responses are inadequate. I believe this is what Jesus would be doing if he was an American today!"

Like Julia, residents of Pilgrim Place in Claremont, California, gather every Friday on the street corner of a busy thoroughfare, holding signs related to the environment, social justice, and immigration. While I was visiting a group gathered for an evening vigil protesting the impeachment acquittal of Donald Trump, one noted, "we need to let the world know that justice is important to us. We need to protest the dishonesty and climate denial of the present administration." These pilgrims reflect the affirmation "picket and pray." I suspect that when many of them set off on peace marches in the area, they feel like Rabbi Abraham Joshua Heschel who asserted after participating in a freedom march with Martin Luther King, "I felt like my legs were praying."

I first met Sue at a vigil in response to the detention of immigrants and the separation of children and their parents at the U.S. southern border. Like many people, including myself, immigration policy has been a call to action, confronting our nation's xenophobia, racism, and violence against the innocent. We have seen Christ in the face of the immigrant child, the Holy Family fleeing to Egypt in families traveling from Central America, and hard-hearted violence of Caesar and Herod in our nation's response, provoking a movement from apathy and hopelessness to agency.

Sue's concern for immigration began a few years before when she relocated, following retirement, to a seacoast community in New England. She discovered that in her idyllic community lived hundreds of legal and undocumented immigrants. While she was unsure how to respond to undocumented immigrants, Sue began to realize that in order maintain their legal status and follow a pathway to citizenship, legal immigrants need to a great deal of support, especially in filling out forms and following immigration procedures. Sue noted that "many of them struggle with the English language, both spoken and written, and the administrative processes necessary to remain legal." In partnership with several other congregations and volunteers for the community, Sue began an immigration task force whose purpose was to welcome and support immigrants and refugees in their township. The committee sought to be holistic in its support of these new Americans, providing furniture, employment counsel, clothing, transportation, and school supplies as well as helping them navigate the immigration bureaucratic procedures.

The emergence of the American border crisis in 2017 challenged Sue to become active in responding to what she describes as the U.S. government's "inhumane separation of toddlers and children from parents, unsafe incarceration, and overall government malpractice." When I looked at their faces on television, "I saw trauma and no light in the eyes of children who should be playing and laughing. I needed to respond. These are God's children, who have done nothing to deserve this punishment." Sue became involved in letter writing and phone campaigns and was instrumental in planning a vigil in New England town. "We can't sit by and let this happen. I see Jesus in each child, and I want to respond with love. I can't let our government become an agent of evil and violence to the innocent."

For Kris, the pivotal moment was the mass shooting at Sandy Hook, December 14, 2012.[5] "It was as she recalls in the middle of Advent, and I tore up my sermon, and began with a reflection on Judith Viorst's children's book *Alexander and the Terrible, Horrible, No Good, Very Bad Day*. I told my congregation that these are the problems Viorst describes—going to the dentist, getting scrunched in the car going to school, falling in a mud puddle, and getting a plain pair of shoes—are the problems first graders should be dealing with and not twenty dead classmates."

Kris knew that she needed to move from preaching to protest and contemplation to action, and the seeds were planted, first, at her church and then in the broader national community, for God Before Guns, an interfaith group, led by Kris and her husband David, whose mission is to be "a multi-faith coalition of individuals and faith communities working to reduce gun injuries and deaths."[6]

Kris retired from full-time congregational ministry in 2015, and notes that "gun violence keeps us very busy. David and I have a great partnership in running the organization." Her husband, David, a retired teacher and teachers union leader, primarily deals legislative issues, while Kris preaches and sponsors events for this growing nonprofit. Now retired, she can focus on one important thing, rather than the many, often conflicting, tasks of congregational ministry. Confronting the 40,000 gun deaths recorded each year in the United States reflects what it means to be a pastor, Kris asserts. "A Christian leader needs to lead. I am still a Christian leader even if I am no longer pastoring a church." Kris's commitment to responding to gun violence, whether mass shootings, suicides, or accidental deaths, is at the heart of what it means for her to follow the way of Jesus. "This isn't political. It's about the sanctity of life, and about not fearing your neighbor enough to arm against them. Jesus didn't back away from controversial issues and neither should we." Although they are suburbanites, Kris and her husband's work to address gun violence has led to greater concern for social justice issues, including gun violence, in inner city Cleveland Kris and many other pastors are experiencing retirement as liberating and enabling them to push the boundaries of social concern and political involvement. Freed from congregational focus, as important as such focus is, they can truly become God's companions in macrocosmic healing.

Bob has had a long career integrating ministry and political involvement.[7] In the 1970s, he served the Carter administration as a speech writer and religious outreach officer. When I spoke with him in his office at the Briggs Center for Faith and Action in Bethesda, Maryland, he had just returned from his annual trip to the Arizona borderlands. For the past ten years, Bob and his wife Linda have journeyed to Sahuarita, Arizona, to work with and learn from the pastor and members of Good Shepherd United Church of Christ. In the most recent visit, he was on a fact-finding tour, learning about immigrants in Nogales, Mexico, who are awaiting entry into the United States. On other journeys, he has been involved in providing water and other necessary supplies along the immigrant trails on the borderlands. Bob laments that the water jugs volunteers leave on immigrant trails are often slashed by vigilantes and border patrol officers. Still, the work must go on. Briggs Center provides clothing, toys, shoes, books, and games Good Shepherd's programs with asylum-seekers and other immigrants.

In the ten years since retirement from full-time ministry, Bob has served as Director of the Briggs Center for Faith and Action, which focuses on immigration, service to the homeless, and education. Currently, the Center provides programs for 300 persons, enrolled in ESOL (English For Speakers of Other Languages), and is on the way to being approved as an Immigration Service Clinic by the Department of Justice, a place where immigrants can receive support and guidance in filling out their immigration applications.[8] At eighty-two, Bob works full time to create programs of hospitality for immigrants and persons in need. On the day we met, he was involved in providing emergency assistance for a refugee from Ethiopia.

For decades, Bob had been involved in the intersection of faith and politics, so it was appropriate when his Baptist congregation merged with the United Church of Christ congregation down the street that the ministry of the church continues in providing social services for immigrants and vulnerable persons. When the church's building was sold, the money was invested in the purchase of a commodious home next door, now called the Carpenter's House, named after the former owner and the Carpenter from Nazareth. Bob asserts that his work is fun, exciting, creative, and does something good for God and others in the world. Bob admitted that he was considering retiring from his position at Briggs Center at eighty-three, and that in the years to come he plans to continue writing and remain active in the community.

Now, in mid-eighties, Ken has slowed down a bit due to health issues.[9] But he still is the social activist I first met in 1979 when I was a newly minted PhD, spending a year in Tucson, Arizona, teaching at Pima Community College and doing my pastoral internship at First Christian Church (Disciples of Christ). When we first met forty years ago, Ken was dealing with the fallout at his church after delivered a stewardship sermon, titled "Getting Off Your Assets." A few years later, Ken became involved in the Sanctuary movement and has never looked back. Looking back over a thirty-five-year ministerial career, Ken avers "we never expected to have refugees knock on our church door and our home." During the height of the Sanctuary movement, Ken was actively involved providing shelter and comfort for undocumented immigrants from Central America. His concern for the Sanctuary movement led him to become involved in the "School of the Americas Watch" initially because of the connection of U.S. imperialism and military training of Central American soldiers with the influx of refugees into the United States. He was later arrested and served six months in prison as a result of his nonviolent civil disobedience at the School of Americas.

Ken is proud of his involvement in starting and serving on the board of Borderlinks, an educational program established in 1989 to "deepen your understanding of borders, migration, and social justice."[10] This program looks at the immigration crisis from a variety of perspectives, including those of Border Patrol officers and undocumented immigrants.

As he reflects on his current social activism, Ken confesses that "I do what I can do." His current health condition has placed limits on his political involvement. Recently, however, when the congregation where he worships, Southside Presbyterian, took in a refugee, he recruited participants for an interfaith service, meeting Monday through Friday at the church. "My limitations won't stop me from doing what I can. I'm a good organizer, and this was something I can do at home."

Jim Antal continues to be a national figure in retirement. Recently retired as Conference Minister for the Massachusetts Conference of the United Church of Christ, Jim recalls that when he was called to the position, he told the committee, "There's just one more thing—I'll need your support to spend at least 10 percent of my time on climate change."[11] Jim has continued crusading for environmental justice since retiring in 2019. His book *Climate Church, Climate World* has become an unexpected best seller and has led to nearly forty speaking engagements since retirement, including talks at the Carter Center in Atlanta, Georgia, and the American Psychiatric Association. He has also been an adviser to the United Nation's Faith for Earth Initiative, whose mission is "the promotion of interreligious and intercultural dialogue, understanding and cooperation for peace."[12] An activist to the core, Jim regularly goes to climate change protests and on occasion is arrested for acts of civil disobedience.

As we shared lunch at a bistro on the edge of the Dartmouth University Campus, Jim was the epitome of a statement affixed to a bench at Kirkridge Retreat and Conference Center, "picket and pray." Jim is a model for acting locally and thinking globally. Active in responding to climate change, he is also getting involved in the politics of his Vermont village, a few miles from Hanover, New Hampshire where we were sharing a meal. Recognizing that responding to climate change is daunting especially when the current U.S. leadership has abandoned the Paris Climate Accord and is rolling back environmental protections, Jim still maintains hope for the future. "Hope," Jim believes, "has nothing to do with optimism. It comes from engagement. Greta Thunberg [the sixteen year old Swedish climate activist] is our teacher. We need to go beyond individual salvation to see salvation as collective, involving the whole earth and its peoples."

THE THREE WISE MEN OF CAPE COD

I intended to meet with Ken, Dave, and Wesley over a supper at a South African restaurant on the Outer Cape, courtesy of the Lilly Endowment and

Louisville Institute. Sadly, the social distancing necessitated by the 2020 Coronavirus (COVID-19) pandemic intervened. Instead I talked with each individually by phone.[13] I have known and respected each of them for several years. They have been leaders in social action across Cape Cod, most particularly as leaders of the Nauset Interfaith Association, a group of twenty-one faith communities in the outer Cape, whose purpose is to "deepen our understanding of each faith group represented; to provide mutual support and encouragement to each other; and to work together for the common good of our community, especially standing with the poor, marginalized, and oppressed."[14]

Ken, now almost eighty, returned "home" to Cape Cod in 2004, where he was ordained to ministry fifty years ago. When he returned to the Cape, Ken "couldn't imagine that a whole new world would open up for him after retirement." No longer active as an Episcopalian priest, he was freed to pursue his passion for social justice and was one of the founding members of the Nauset Interfaith Association. "I am grateful for the church that nurtured my spirituality, but I am glad to be outside institutional structures and issues of congregational survival to focus on the wider world." Passionate for justice, Ken has been active in working for the common good, especially in relationship to issues of justice, racism, and environmental concerns. Both Cape Codders, we talked about the importance of a bill in Massachusetts House to ban the use of plastic water bottles. Like his two friends and colleagues, Ken recognizes the broader relationship between issues of justice, economics, racism, and the environment. Ken states that he finds hope in "my experience with persons of other faiths and outside the church working on issues of the common good." Ken noted that "nearly eighty, I still have passion and it is strengthened by justice-centered relationships."

Ordained a deacon in the United Methodist Church nearly sixty years ago, Dave retired to Cape Cod fifteen years ago. Dave notes that "being retired allowed me to be a social activist. It liberated me from the politics of congregational life." His main retirement focus has been on the MLK Action Team, sponsored by the Nauset Interfaith Association. "Being part of the MLK Team has kept me sharp. I have been involved working with police chiefs in the Outer Cape. Our goal has been to nurture relationships, listen to one another, share our concerns related to racist behaviors, and hear the struggles that police officers have on Cape Cod."

Such conversations are holy in nature, despite their secular context. They enable different groups to empathize with one another and go beyond stereotypes based on race and profession.

Since 2004, Dave and his wife Pam have been actively involved in curating the histories of some of the lesser known heroes of the civil rights movement. A gifted artist, Pam has created icons of these hidden figures of the civil rights movement, while Dave has told their stories. Dave and Pam note that "it is our conviction that the efforts that they made in the cause of justice will be lost if their stories are not written down and remembered . . . we must not forget those 'ordinary people who did such extraordinary things.'"[15]

Committed to Martin Luther King's vision of the Beloved Community, Dave struggles to maintain hope in the era of Trump. "For the past few years, I've had a pit in my stomach. I find hope in working with others to seek justice and combat both implicit and explicit racism of our nation." Dave also finds hope in humor, even in a time of pandemic. Humor gives us perspective even in challenging times.

Wesley has spent four decades as a congregational pastor, campus minister, minister of racial issues and urban minister, and district superintendent for the New England Conference of the United Methodist Church. After retiring from a United Methodist congregation on Cape Cod, Wesley became a key leader of the MLK Action Team of the Nauset Interfaith Association, focusing on race relations of Cape Cod and responding to both subtle and overt racism. He has been the coordinator of nearly twenty congregations studying Martin Luther King's "Letter from the Birmingham Jail." Wesley believes that one of the fruits of this study will be finding ways to "take direct action against racism on Cape Cod." Wesley experiences hope in "repairing the racial divide on Cape Cod. More people are interested in race relations than I realized. I hope for a new tapestry of relationships to tap into culture of change."

Dave, Ken, and Wesley are three wise men of Cape Cod. In retirement, they like so many of the ministers with whom I spoke see themselves as activists seeking to build bridges among persons and heal the soul of America. In the spirit of the prophets and Jesus, they seek to embody God's Shalom "on earth as it is in heaven."

PATHWAYS TO JUBILEE

In the intricate interdependence of life, we are blessed to be a blessing to others. Our vocation involves joining our gifts with the world's needs and claiming our place as God's companions in healing the world. In every season of life, we can do something beautiful for God, and in taking our role to further the moral arc of the universe, we experience greater joy and fulfillment. When we discover our deep joy, we discover with Eric Liddell from "Chariots of Fire" that "God made me fast and when I run, I can feel God's pleasure." Where are you feeling God's pleasure and how will you share that divine pleasure as a retired pastor?

Examen of Gifts for Ongoing Service

In this spiritual exercise, we will explore our gifts in the spirit of the Examen that we have employed throughout this text.

1. After a time of stillness, give thanks for the wondrous world that sustains you and your family in body, mind, spirit, and relationships. Affirm generous interdependence of life, grounded in God's graceful providence and embodied your unique gifts. Give thanks for your life and the blessings you have received.
2. Prayerfully review your gifts and passions. What gets you up in the morning? What activities energize and empower you to help others? What pastoral activities still energize you? What activities are you passionate about?
3. Notice your attitudes toward your gifts and talents, which ones are most in synch with your relationship with God?
4. Identify the needs of those around you, interpersonal, local, and global, connecting them with your gifts and passions. Toward what forms of ministry, in the broadest sense of the word, do these gifts and passions lead you?
5. Look toward the future with gratitude and resolve to move forward in connecting your gifts, life situation, health with the needs of the world around you.

Conclude your Examen with a prayer such as: *Loving God, thank you for the giftedness of life and your gifts moving in my life. Awaken me to new gifts and possibilities and give me the insight and energy to use my gifts to be your companion in healing the world. In Christ's Name. Amen.*

Imaging Your Future

Most of the pastors with whom I conversed began visualizing their retirement while they were still actively involved in pastoral ministry, whether in a parish, conference, institutional, or academic setting. They asked themselves questions such as: What do I plan to do to continue serving during retirement? Where is God calling me next in ministry? What new mission is God calling me toward? What best reflects my current level of energy and creativity? Many of these pastors also recognized that they might need a sabbatical from volunteer and service work to regain their sense of health and well-being, recover from the stresses of ministry, or discover their new identity in retirement.

In this exercise, set aside time for reflection over a month-long period, focusing on the question "Where is God calling me to serve?" Without any clear sense of destination or goal, let your mind wander, free-associating, and letting images come to mind in response to the prayer, "God, show me how I can serve the world in this new season of life?"

Take time to visualize the contours of the calling toward which you are led. What adventures will you have? What challenges? Whom will you meet and how will your life be transformed?

After each session, set aside time to write down any insights that emerge from your visualizations. These can be the basis for charting the pathway to your next adventure in healing the world, whether it involves spending time with grandchildren, challenging unjust social structures, volunteering at hospice, or supporting undocumented workers.

The Center Is Everywhere

One of my favorite descriptions of God, articulated by Bonaventure, Nicolas of Cusa and others is: "God is a circle whose center is everywhere and whose circumference is nowhere." Every person and place is at the center of God's presence and activity. You are at the center of God's care. God loves each of us as God's beloved child. The divine circumference is all-encompassing, centering all of us in love. Service takes us from self-preoccupation to embrace larger and larger circles of love, beginning with friends, family, and fellow citizens and encompassing the world. In this exercise, I invite you to explore the ever-expanding circles of God's love and your role as God's companion in healing the world.

Begin with a time of gentle breathing, focusing your attention on God's energy entering and energizing you. Visualize God's light entering and filling you with each breath and surrounding you in a permeable and protective "armor of light" (Romans 13:12). Experience God's presence within you as you inhale and, in a similar manner, exhale God's presence, connecting you with the world beyond. Let each breath contribute to the well-being of the world beyond yourself. Experience the light comes from you as healing those whom you visualize. Let the light emerging in your own life grow in ever-expanding circles, beginning with intimate friends and family, your congregation, your community, state, nation, and planet. Feel your connection with the human and nonhuman world. Let this connection expand to include the whole earth and beyond. Then, visualize this light circling back toward you from the edges of your experience to your personal center. Conclude with a prayer for the graceful and healing interconnectedness of life, and your vocation as God's companion in tikkun 'olam, healing the world.

A Prayer for the Pathway. Light of the world, breathe in and through me, filling me with your loving light. Let your light shine in and through me to embrace the whole earth. Let my light bring life and love to the world. In Christ's Love. Amen.

NOTES

1. Jean-Pierre de Caussade, *The Sacrament of the Present Moment* (New York: Harper San Francisco, 1982), 1, 17.
2. Ibid., 15.
3. https://journaltherapy.com/
4. Real name.
5. Real name.
6. godbeforeguns.org
7. Real name.
8. briggscenter.org
9. Real name.
10. https://www.borderlinks.org/
11. Jim Antal, *Climate Church, Climate World: How People of Faith Must Work for Change* (Lanham, MD: Rowman & Littlefield, 2018), 139.
12. https://www.unenvironment.org/about-un-environment/faith-earth-initiative
13. Real names.
14. https://nausetinterfaith.org
15. Pamela Chatterton-Purdy and David Purdy, *Icons of the Civil Rights Movement: Dispelling White Privilege* (Barnstable, MA: West Barnstable Press, 2016).

Chapter 10

Necessary Losses

Aging, Grief, and Death

> So we do not lose heart. Even though our outer nature is wasting away, our inner nature is being renewed day by day. For this slight momentary affliction is preparing us for an eternal weight of glory beyond all measure, because we look not at what can be seen but at what cannot be seen; for what can be seen is temporary, but what cannot be seen is eternal. (II Corinthians 4:16–18)

Over forty years ago, I recall George Tolman, Senior Pastor of First Christian Church (Disciples of Christ), who was my field education mentor, describing the reality of death in a sermon: "Life is risky business. No one gets out alive. The mortality rate will always be 100%." Once robust and vital, but now living with chronic leukemia, Jack, a retired United Church of Christ pastor, now in his seventies, quipped, "Good health is merely the slowest possible rate at which one can die!"

Surely, aging, grief, and death, are the "necessary losses" we must all face, unless we die at childbirth. Now, at sixty-seven, I can joke that "I am in still in mid-life provided I live to be 134!" In joking about my age, my words take the edge off my own aging process and always get a laugh, but there is a trace of gallows human in my commentary: I'm not fooling anyone, myself included. I am mortal. I'm unlikely despite hip replacements, better living through medication, and good health habits to make it past 100, and there is something sobering about that recognition. The current Coronavirus epidemic, occurring as I write these lines, has only exacerbated my sense of mortality and the mortality of those who have shared their stories in this text.

I feel vital intellectually and can still bind up the stairs. But, I'm not as agile as I imagine myself to be on a good day and don't recover as well from injury as I did at thirty. Although I am active, physically, professionally, and mentally, I take medications daily and pause when I hear of a colleague or classmate dying in their sixties and early seventies. As a village pastor, I peruse the local obituaries daily as part of my pastoral routine, and note peoples' age and cause of death, knowing that sometime in the future my name will be listed among the obituaries. As I hear eulogies at funerals and memorial services, I now ponder what my colleagues, congregants, friends, and family might say about me. I wonder what the preacher's funeral sermon will be when I am finally laid to rest! When I see that a theologian or celebrity dies at eighty-seven or ninety-three, or in their seventies, I reflect for a moment about whether I have ten, twenty, or twenty-five good years left, with the emphasis on "good years."

This Fall morning as I was walking on the parking lot at Craigville Beach, I stepped on a depression in the pavement and twisted my ankle. This is not particularly remarkable in and of itself. Although I was grateful that I did not sustain a serious injury, this is the second time in the past two weeks I have stepped on a rock or depression and narrowly avoided a break. While any physiological basis for these incidents is unlikely, nevertheless they gave me pause. Will I become one of these elders who walks in circles on the indoor track at the Rec Center or Mall to avoid falling? Will I be perambulating with a walker and cane someday rather than fast-walking on the beach? My feelings of concern were exacerbated by my noticing a floater in my vision the previous day, the first eye issue I have experienced. I realize I am among the "worried well" and am grateful for my overall good health and intellectual acuity. Still, I wonder: Is this the beginning of a gradual decline toward decrepitude? Recognizing life's synchronicities as well as the realities of chance, along with the challenges of the current pandemic, I was consoled that my musings were interrupted by the refrain of Bob Marley's "Three Little Birds" on the radio, telling me not to worry, because everything is going to be alright!

As pastors, we recognize that aging and death are essential aspects of our work. We are all too familiar with declining and dying senior adults, with once-vital ninety-year-olds sliding downhill in the space of a few months with little or no reason, other than aging itself. Such realities often lead to difficult conversations regarding aging in place or moving into a nursing home or assisted living.

In the course of my ministry, like most pastors, I have visited many congregants on the last few days of their lives and memorial services are major part of my ministry on Cape Cod, "the Florida of the Northeast."

My own aging process reminds me of Martin Luther's words on the reality of death, "In the midst of life, we are surrounded by death. In the midst of death, we are surrounded by life." Life is beautiful but all too brief. I ponder Mary Oliver's comment about the brevity of life and then her question to herself as much as her readers, what will you do with your unique, wonderful, and amazing life?

We are star stuff, the children of the first day of creation, containing within us the image of God, embodied in unfettered imagination and all-encompassing compassion. The Love that created the universe flows through us, but only for a little while in this precious and unique lifetime. As Jewish wisdom notes: everyone should have a note in each pocket, with the first note affirming, "For you the universe was made," its companion reminding, "You are dust to dust you will return."

"All things must pass," late Beatle George Harrison noted. In the 13.8 billion-year journey of this universe, decorated with a trillion galaxies, each with a hundred billion suns, and planets revolving around billions of these suns, all things have an expiration date, even our 4.5 billion-year-old planet Earth.

Mortality and suffering are sources of theological reflection and are at the heart of pastoral ministry. They strike fear in our hearts, but also inspire compassion and activism, and the affirmation that "This is the day that God has made. Let us rejoice and be glad in it." In this brief and unrepeatable day—this short lifetime—our calling is to do something beautiful for God and claim our place in all our finitude and fallibility as God's companions in healing the earth.

We cannot avoid the challenges of necessary losses, whether these involve physical vitality, relational changes brought on by the death of loved ones, and our own eventual deaths. These may turn our world upside down, forcing us to let go of the familiar as we venture, often without our consent, to the uncharted territories that accompany the aging process. Letting go of the familiar can be disorienting; it can also be an invitation to new horizons. Novelties abound and they call us to be creative, initiating our own novel behaviors in response to the unfamiliar territories through which we must journey.

A retired Episcopalian pastor, Steven, discovered one night that the contemplation of death can deaden our spirits or awaken us to live each day fully. Awakening in the early hours of the morning, Steven recalls that "I thought I would die that night, and there was nothing I could do about it! I would go to sleep and not wake up! You can imagine how grateful I was to awaken the next morning." That sobering experience was a wake up call: that changed his life dramatically. "I could no longer put off till tomorrow what I needed to do today. I didn't have forever. Death could come at any moment and I wanted to live. I had put off so much in ministry. It was good work, but it enveloped my life and left me little emotional energy for parenting and marriage. But, now was the time to change," this seventy-year-old pastor realized. "I take each day as it comes, delighting in it, spending time with loved ones, and getting out there to make a difference." Steve has deepened his relationship with his wife, much to her surprise and joy, and is spending as much time as possible with his grandchildren and their parents. "Death woke me up to life, and its preciousness, and I will live as fully as I can until the day I die."

LIVING EACH DAY

Two contrasting images emerged as I was conducting interviews on clergy retirement. About half the people I spoke with had recently or were preparing for a surgical procedure. I heard stories about stents and bypasses and knee and hip replacements, tough recoveries and greater agility and energy. I also heard affirmations that life is full of possibilities and that we have more to do in retirement than we imagined. Like Jacob, many of us limp through the day. Yet, we are also, in our spirits and life involvements, still full of vigor. We may move more slowly and no longer bound down the stairs at home, but we are also inspired to face the day with hopeful expectation and challenging possibility. With Isaiah 40:31, our spirits are vital despite physical limits:

Those who wait for the LORD shall renew their strength,
they shall mount up with wings like eagles,
they shall run and not be weary,
they shall walk and not faint.

The aging process brings on a series of "new normals" and limitations, and yet within the concrete limits of life new possibilities are also birthed. Physical diminishment may be accompanied by a sense of constriction as we count our days in terms of doctor's appointments. Aging may also turn us toward what is truly important in life. Numbering our days may lead to a heart of wisdom as we ground in perspective, trusting God and coming to affirm, despite the inevitable challenges of the aging process:

So we do not lose heart. Even though our outer nature is wasting away, our inner nature is being renewed day by day. For this slight momentary affliction is preparing us for an eternal weight of glory beyond all measure, because we look not at what can be seen but at what cannot be seen; for what can be seen is temporary, but what cannot be seen is eternal. (2 Corinthians 4:16–18)

The apostle Paul is a realist. There is no denial of age and diminishment. There is also a deeper realism, inspired by his hope in the unseen and eternal. Beneath limitation is the horizon of everlasting life, bringing with it a recognition that we can experience abundant life in the midst of change because God is our faithful companion.

Lynn experiences the interplay of despair and hope in her response to the diminishment of aging. In the course of my conversations with Lynn, a retired Unitarian Universalist pastor in her late sixties, she noted "recovery is a lot slower these days." She was about to begin a regimen of physical therapy as part of her healing from fall-related shoulder surgery. Over the past several years, Lynn has taught congregational-based courses in death and dying and has been a hospice volunteer in the area of music therapy. She thinks about death a lot these days, not only because of her professional interests and experience as a hospice chaplain but as a result of a series of difficult health issues, including the emergence of autoimmune disease. Put starkly, Lynn asserts "aging leads to death." Lynn's aging process has been complicated by financial issues. She retired early due to health issues and has been unable to find any part-time or occasional pastoral or hospice opportunities in her area. Lynn confesses that for a while, "I found myself at near poverty, not able to cover basics, let alone thrive." Given her current health and relationship status—Lynn is currently single—Lynn has lots of questions, "Will I die earlier than I thought I would when I was in midlife? Will I die alone? If I become infirm, will I spend the rest of my life in a nursing home because I have no one to provide basic care?"

Lynn also finds herself "mourning the fact that she is no longer active in ministry." Her volunteer leadership of a midweek service at her local church is the high point of her week. By her own admission, "I have so much to give, and yet right now, due to health and location, I am unable live out my vocation."

Despite her current physical infirmities and their impact on her sense of well-being and hope, Lynn persists in deepening her spiritual life. Lynn states that she "prays for discernment every day." Her own process of discernment has enabled her to face death square in the face, while treasuring every day. "Illness is a call to think about our deaths. Eventually we have to let go of everything familiar. We need to ask 'do we need this possession or family heirloom any more?' as we simplify our lives so that we can focus on what is truly important."

Lynn has embarked on a process of letting go similar in nature to the process of Hinduism's four stages of life. In Hindu spirituality, the first two stages involve acquisition of education, professional skills, status, and property. The third and fourth stages of life focus on what Carl Jung would describe as spiritual individuation or wholeness: the stage forest dweller, a time of retirement and simplification, and the final stage, sannyasi, which focuses on preparing for death and with it union with the Divine. In her own words, "I have experienced letting go of health, professional life, possessions. I know that someday I will need to let go of my life as well." Although sometimes she is "in the pits," Lynn still has hope, grounded in her spiritual life and her trust that, despite current health problems, she may be able practice ministry once more, ideally in a quarter time position at a church or hospice. Through it all, Lynn is guided by the words of Psalm 90:12: "So teach us to count our days so that we may gain a wise heart." As she looks toward the future, Lynn admits that pastors "need to be giving and need to be needed. I still have so much to give." Her current ability to give to her community through creative worship and her hopes for physical recovery motivate her to run the race with realism and courage.

Jack noted that "my life is spent between visits to the doctor. That leaves me weary and sometimes depressed. After fifty years of ministry, I'm at the sidelines and can't even go to church on a regular basis. Now, I'm on the prayer list and my pastor visits me! I still have something to share, and most of that occurs on Facebook now."

The day after we spoke, Jack posted the following statement on Facebook: "Grant me daily the grace of gratitude, to be thankful for all my gifts, and so be freed from artificial needs, so that I might lead a joyful, simple life."

Chris told me that her motto in retirement is "she persisted." Active in local politics and national justice issues, Chris wakes every morning with pain. "It seems," she noted, "that some months my life is punctuated by medical appointments—family practitioner, dermatologist, ophthalmologist, dentist, spine doctor, orthopedist, and physical therapist. I try to keep a good spirit, but some days I want to stay in bed. But, then, the world calls me—the cries of children on the borderlands, bullying of LGBTQ+ persons, racism in the seats of power and in our town, and of course, my grandchildren and their families." Although she has a supportive husband, Chris still struggles with physical pain and the accompanying impatience that goes with it. But, "still I persist. I am needed at home and in politics. I can't give up. I can't turn my back on God's call."

For many pastors, aging brings both fatigue and generativity. Losing a step or two does not bring depression, but a pervasive commitment to "creative immortality" and "generativity," as Robert Jay Lifton and Erik Erikson describe the tasks of midlife and aging. When I recently spoke with Drew, he noted that there had been "a lot of personal stuff on his plate. We are the older generation, and I am the youngest child in my family of several siblings and aunts and uncles. I am seeing a lot of sickness and death these days. When our peers are beginning to die, it is a constant reminder of the season we are in."

Drew noted the unique challenges pastors face as they live out their aging process, "On the one hand, we are spiritual leaders and people still look to us for comfort and hope even after we leave the parish. On the other hand, we are often grieving ourselves and can't be professionals in our own grieving and dying process."

Sometimes the realities of aging are simply fatiguing, Drew admits. Drew and his wife had just returned from several days with his sister, who had been on death's door, but miraculously recovered. "We're tired and need a respite ourselves. We need everyone to be healthy for a while."

As a pastor and one of the few religiously oriented persons in his family, Drew has become his family's tribal priest, officiating at weddings and funerals. These experiences often provoke deep emotions. Drew found himself verklempt at a recent family funeral, when he observed one of his aunts, now in her eighties, fixing her gaze on him. "I seemed to know what she was thinking: here's this grey-haired, grey-bearded preacher, and I remember him when he as a little boy in short pants." Now in his late sixties, Drew anticipates a slew of memorial services lying ahead for him. "Nothing like dying relatives to remind you of your own mortality," he noted. Drew also noted that he has begun to consider his legacy and the legacy of his generation for his grandchildren and future generations. He reminded me, "Bruce, we're from the same generation. Anti-war, ecology, summer of love. We had a dream of a different world. Now I wonder what we will leave the next generations."

In an interdependent universe, nothing is ever lost, our lives radiate, for good or ill beyond ourselves, giving us a sense of continuity and immortality beyond our lifetimes. Both of us pondered the question, "Have we been good stewards? Can we overcome our errors and leave a better future for those who come after us?" For Drew, the interplay of limitation and legacy has made time precious. "I don't mess around, I don't waste time, I need to get down to the business of doing what I can in seeking justice and democracy in our nation and combating the dangers of global climate change. I don't believe that God will rescue us from our folly and greed. The future we leave is what our children and God will have to work with, and I want to leave a hopeful future for the generations to come."

While everlasting life is in God's hands, we are responsible to live out our vocation as God's companions in healing the world, letting go of our own narrow self-interest to focus on planetary well-being and community healing.

LIVING WITH LOSS

Throughout this book, I have invoked Judith Viorst's images of life's "necessary losses." For many years, I have assigned C. S. Lewis's memoir of his grief experience following the death of his wife Joy from as a text in death and dying and narrative theology courses. Lewis notes:

> For all pairs of lovers without exception, bereavement is a universal and integral part of our experience of love. It follows marriage normally as marriage follows

courtship and as autumn follows summer. It is not a truncation of the process but one of its phases; not the interruption of the dance, but the next figure. We are "taken out of ourselves" by the loved one while she is here. Then comes the tragic figure of the dance in which we must need to be still taken out of ourselves through the bodily presence is withdrawn, to love the very Her, and not fall back to loving our past, or our memory, or our sorrow, or our relief from sorrow, or our own love.[1]

Kate and I have been married over forty years, through youth, parenting, midlife, and now grandparenting. We have many years to look forward to following retirement, at least that is our hope. But still our time together is finite, and eventually one of us will go on without the other. Neither one of us accept the quip, attributed to a man reflecting the impact of mortality on marriage, "if one of us dies, I'll go to Paris." There is no "if" about it; nor is there any clarity as to who will stay and who will leave. In my own family, the expectation was that my dad, who was almost a decade older than my mom, would go first. In fact, he lived thirteen years after her death.

When my mother died in 1980, my pastor-father wondered why it was not him. He was nearly ten years older, and he always thought he would be the first to go. After forty-four years of marriage, he initially found it difficult to go on. Their lives had been intertwined by domestic and relational rituals—trips to the shopping center, gardening, favorite television shows, going to church, and devotional reading. At eighty, my father did not believe he had much to give to the world. Then, after a few months, he took up one of my mother's retirement vocations—reaching out to the homebound of our church with phone calls and cards. After my father died, I discovered his prayer list of over twenty people. I had not realized that he and my mom regularly prayed for persons they perceived in need of spiritual or physical healing. My father found his healing from grief in sharing in the healing of others and in caring for my brother who struggled with mental health issues. He never quit mourning my mom, but in the next several years he found peace in his mourning by continuing the ministry of care that had characterized his life for over four decades. Like Dorothy Day, whose declining process kept her from attending speaking engagements and getting arrested protests, my Dad learned that his vocation was simply to pray. My father grieved deeply but found meaning in prayer, writing poetry, and caring for others.

Eventually all good marriages involve the death of one of the partners. As C. S. Lewis avers, grief is a season in marriage, just as significant as falling in love, raising children, and growing old together. Several of the pastors with whom I spoke noted the pain of losing their spouse. For most, grief is a spiritual issue that stretches and grows their faith. There are many pathways to going through the valley of grief, but as one pastor noted "painful as it is, grief must be faced, not just for ourselves but for our families and those who have looked up to us."

Another pastor asserted, "it's tough being single; she was truly my other half, and for a while I felt lost. But I discovered that the spiritual practices that sustained me throughout my life—prayer and meditation—helped me deal with the loss of my wife and enabled me to reinvest in relationships."

A Canadian pastor noted that "the grief was awful at first, but it passed and now I feel free as a single person to pursue whatever callings God has in store for me now." While many pastors remarry, this eighty-five-year old pastor is content with being single and "following my path, God's path for me, at this point of my life."

A resident of Pilgrim Place noted "I expected to go first. But, she died two years ago. Now what?" He has found a new life writing, doing pottery, and reaching out to the homeless of idyllic Claremont. His tablemate, another widower, continued: "When she died, a part of me died, too. It was hard. But, I've found that I love my own company. I'm active in the community. But I enjoy being alone, reflecting and reading." Life involves letting go and the loss may be unbearable but as the apostle Paul notes in our weakness, we may discover the power of God to transform our lives and give us a hopeful future.

THE VITALITY OF DEATH

A seminary student, in the middle of his first field education assignment, confessed, "I didn't know that ministry involves so much death and dying." Perhaps he imagined that ministry was primarily about preaching and mission. He was surprised to find out that every week most pastors deal with issues of serious illness, aging, family conversations about elderly parents, visiting the death bed, comforting mourners, and planning funerals and memorial services. A plaque at Paris Hospital soberly reminded health care providers, "We are the dying caring for the dying." The same maxim is addressed to ministers, "we the dying pastoring to the dying."

Death can paralyze or energize. One of my favorite spiritual stories involves Gautama's call to seek enlightenment. Raised in privilege, he had never encountered the shadow side of life. His father surrounded him with health, wealth, and pleasure as a way of preventing him from fulfilling a childbirth prophesy that he would be great spiritual leader and not his father's successor to the throne. But, in the course of three days, Gautama ventured forth from the palace and encountered an old person, a sick person, and a corpse. Shaken, he left the palace on the fourth day and encountered a monk, whose presence inspired him to abandon royalty in the quest for enlightenment.

As I noted earlier, now that I am in my late sixties, mortality has become a daily experience for me. I am numbering my days in relationship to the longevity of others. I note obituaries and do the math: how old was the deceased and how many years do I have until I reach that age? Or, when I see the *Christian Century* death notices of an eminent theologian, pastor, or denominational leader, I wander, "will I make it to my late eighties? That's only twenty years. It seems like a long time." Then, I remember my father in his eighties noting "how quickly it goes" or the words of congregants looking back on eight or nine decades and wondering where the time went and pondering how many Christmases lie ahead for them.

This morning as I was preparing to begin my daily ritual of writing 500 to 1,000 words, I observed another predawn ritual—a strong cup of coffee. I have dozens of coffee cups on my shelf and most days, I randomly choose one, many of which provide an inspirational saying to begin the day. This morning, as I was thinking about mortality, I picked up a cup that announced God's promise to Jeremiah. Under the heading "Journey," the cup proclaimed "For I know the plans I have for you, plans to prosper you and not to harm you, plans to give you hope and a future" (Jeremiah 29:11). This promise seemed highly synchronous as I reflected on my own death and the deaths of my loved ones. God is faithful, seeking our well-being, in all the seasons of life!

As a college sophomore, almost fifty years ago, I enrolled in a course taught by one of San Jose State's most popular professors, Peter Koestenbaum. The Vietnam War was still raging, students were protesting the ROTC facilities on campus, and classes were regularly halted with faux bomb threats. A course on existentialism seemed appropriate at the time as nineteen- and twenty-year-old students pondered the meaning of life in the context of pervasive threats of death and the realities of social change. The one required textbook was Koestenbaum's *The Reality of Death.*[2] Koestenbaum alerted us that despite our youth, we were mortal, and that embracing our mortality was not only frightening but also liberating. Facing death, our own deaths, and the deaths of others could energize, empower, and enlighten us, and challenge us to put first things first. In this one amazing and unique life, death constantly queries, what will you do to add to the beauty, love, and goodness of the world. The reality of death is not accompanied with an instruction book, describing how we will find meaning, it simply announces, "life is precious and find a path that nourishes your soul and the lives of others." As William Saroyan counsels in the prologue to his play, "The Time of Your Life": "In the time of your life, live—so that in that wondrous time you shall not add to the misery and sorrow of the world, but shall smile to the infinite delight and mystery of it."[3]

As he looks toward the future, Bill (mentioned earlier) admits that "life is very different than he imagined." A second-career pastor, Tom and his wife

Karen planned for a financially stable retirement, enabling them to enjoy travel, leisurely visits with their children and grandchildren, and then relocate to the East Coast to be nearer their three children and five grandchildren. They were on the road to the retirement toward which they planned when Karen was diagnosed with Alzheimer's disease. Now, her diminishment and eventual death is a daily reality, shaping virtually every aspect of Tom's life. The reality of her death and his need to remain healthy and strong has deepened his sense of call, this time, to a different kind of ministry, the ministry of faithfulness and love.

"I made a vow," seventy-year-old Bill asserted as we talked about how his wife Karen's Alzheimer's disease has changed their relationship. "For better for worse and in sickness and in health. Now I'm living that out." While she is in early stages, the disease has shaped their relationship and the way Bill relates to the world. "She's happy, and I'm thankful for that. But, she doesn't talk much anymore. Most of the time we just sit side by side, keeping company with each other. I feel like my life could be the final scene from the movie "The Color Purple"—the couple sitting on the porch, rocking our chairs, and gazing in the distance."

Karen's disease, Bill admits, has taught him some essential life lessons. "Death has clarified my values and shown me what is truly important in life. I'm more patient now. I'm just frustrated at times, but I try not to take it out on Karen. I have learned to live in the moment. Now is the only time we have, and even when I'm planning for the future, it's in the here and now."

A lifelong planner, who enjoys familiar rituals, Bill notes that he has "come to live with uncertainty. While Karen is currently in pretty good shape, everything could change without notice, and I need to let go of the future, trusting that God is with us and will give me the resources I need to be faithful and caring."

He has also discovered that the heart is more important than the mind at this time of their relationship. "It really doesn't matter now what I say, or if Karen understands it, but how I say it and now I bring joy to her life by being loving and attentive with the simple things."

While living in the now, Bill is pondering whether—or when—he and Karen should move East where their three children live. Her diminishment and his aging may lead to a time when he needs to reach out to others, to the larger village to help them navigate the next stage of their relationship. "I know we will have to do this eventually, and though we're fine now, I don't want to wait till it's too late for either one or both of us." His experience with his wife's Alzheimer's and the daily reality of her—and now his—mortality has inspired Bill to "live in the now. The future isn't promised to either of us. Just this moment, and I want to make it a beautiful one for us. In my prayers, I open to God's peace regardless of what the future brings. I trust what I believed before Karen's diagnosis: The Sacred is present. Love is present. In all the changes we've faced, one thing doesn't—the Sacred is here with us."

Bill has hope in the future, and his hope is in God's love which replenishes his own finite love and provides him with the resources of a power greater than his own.

Newly remarried and on the verge of his sixty-eighth birthday, Roy, a Pennsylvania United Church of Christ pastor, spoke of death and new life. Recently retired after nearly forty years of congregational ministry, he now works part-time as a hospice chaplain. In many ways, a youthful experience prepared him for his next step in ministry: at twenty-four he nearly died as the result of a head-on collision. He vowed after he recovered, to "never waste a day." Over forty years later, he carried that same spirit, and he meets each day with a healthy agnosticism. "Mystery and wonder are the abiding principles of my spiritual life. His work at hospice has only increased his sense of wonder and my joy in relationships with my wife, children, and grandchildren. I try never to miss anything, and I feel that there's still so much to learn about God, myself, and the world."

"Hospice has showed me that everyone has a story. My task is simply to listen, to ask questions, and help people find their voice in telling their stories. In hearing their stories, I am discovering anew my own story, and my own role in the scheme of things."

Sondra, a West Coast United Methodist pastor, now in her fifth year of retirement treasures each day. "I believe we are part of an eternal journey. I trust the future to God and believe that God will be with me when I die. I was raised believing in a literal heaven and hell, but now I see the afterlife in terms of what people are reporting in near death experiences, healing the past, meeting loved ones, and encountering Jesus. I recently picked up some of the work of Leslie Weatherhead, the British Methodist pastor and writer, and am pondering the possibility of some form of reincarnation."[4] I am not afraid of death, though the dying process gives me pause. I'm single now, and don't have children, so I wonder how I will get along if I become disabled. Still, whatever the future brings, I trust God.

Sondra takes solace in the words of the apostle Paul, "If we live, we live to God, and if we die, we die to God; so then, whether we live or whether we die, we are God's" (Romans 14:8).

Now in his mid-seventies, Henry sees his own death in theological terms. He recalled the death of his mother at age ninety-five last year, "When her physician asked her how long she wanted to live, she answered, 'I want to live forever.'" Henry believes he will live forever. He sees death as part of a process of spiritual evolution. "Life is full of transitions. I don't think about death too often. I don't think of beginnings and endings, but in terms of change and transformation. The afterlife, for me, is a matter of moving on.

The quality of our afterlife reflects our spiritual consciousness and involves growing in our awareness of God's presence in our lives."

Like his mother, he wants to continue for a few more decades. "There is so much to do. So many books to read. There is so much to learn and I want to learn as much in this lifetime before I continue my growth in Eternity." While Henry believes that we can learn a great deal about the afterlife from near death, paranormal, and mystical experiences, he recognizes that God is the Mystery that beckons us forward. Citing one of his favorite scripture verses, "we walk by faith and not by sight" (2 Corinthians 5:7). In the meantime, "we need to grow as much as we can in this wonderful life and trust the process of spiritual evolution to God."

George also sees death and dying in theological terms.[5] The process theology that has guided his personal and professional life also guides his reflections on mortality. An elder statesman in the United Church of Canada, he shared that he and his wife had just sold their lovely river home in Ontario, a place I had visited on several occasion for holiday and speaking engagements, and were embarking on a move across country to Vancouver Island. He was looking forward to the next adventure but was also dealing with the challenges of downsizing. "The hard part of downsizing is deciding what to give away. Our new place is much smaller, so I have had to give away 25 boxes of books. My wife and I are only taking three boxes with us. In giving away these books, a history of my life is disappearing."

Now almost eighty, George and his wife Suzanne felt the need to move closer their children. "Finding the right time is a challenge, and this is the right time. While we're still healthy and can make the trip on our own." In addition to his books, "George had to go through over fifty years of papers—seminary notes, sermons, and research."

When I asked him about mortality, George responded, "I know I'm going to die. It's not a big deal." A process theologian, George considers aging to be an adventure. He is content with mortality, realizing that how we live in this life, the present moment and the legacy we leave, is what is most important. "Life after death doesn't interest me. Life before death interests me. I want to live as long as I have all my capabilities and am not a burden to my family. Death is not something I fight. Life is something I treasure. I don't look forward to the afterlife. Being part of God's memory is enough for me and making my contribution to the lives of others is reward enough. The reward is being alive today, doing my part, and bringing beauty to the world. Still, even though I don't need eternal life, I may just be surprised."

In his early sixties and facing death from chronic heart disease, Art celebrates life. In fact, he recently remarried. He and his wife "want to grow old together" despite his prognosis. Guided by his faith, Art affirms that "honoring Jesus has always been my goal in life. I am not frightened about death. It will be a transition from here to eternal life. I believe that nothing can separate me from the love of God. I don't know the details, that's in God's hands. It is difficult for me to believe that my experience and creativity will be snuffed out at death."

The reality of death has inspired Art to live in the now. "Jan and I are hoping to make memories in the time we have together, perhaps no more than five years. We are planning a trip to Montreal. I am seeing my kids and grandkids more." Art wants to be remembered, and hope that I live long enough for my young grandchildren, now nine and seven to remember me. "I am making videos for the grands. I want them to remember me. I will leave these videos as a witness to my values." Art worries about the dying process. "People with my illness often feel like they are drowning and gasping for air and that frightens me. I want to die with dignity. So I hope for a sudden heart attack. Still, I trust God with the future, and hold on to the promise that God is with me whatever comes."

There is no avoiding death. Our hope is that we can experience God's presence and rejoice in the time of our lives, remembering that "this is the day God has made."

PATHWAYS TO JUBILEE

I must admit that aging and dying do not seem like a jubilee. Still, although we are surrounded by death, as Luther says, we can claim life in its abundance not as observers but as actors who add to the beauty and love of the world. Each day matters and our lives can be a witness to our values and our commitments to be God's partners in healing the earth.

Listening to Your Eulogy

Over my forty years of ministry, I have heard hundreds of funeral and memorial service eulogies given by children, grandchildren, coworkers, siblings, and friends. Eulogies then to highlight certain aspects of the deceased character, relationships, or values. As I reach my late sixties, the issue of eulogies is more personal than it was when I was in my twenties. Eulogies are a testimony to "creative" or "objective" immortality, our impact on life beyond ourselves.

In the spirit of Rabbi Hillel's counsel, "If not now, when?" reflect on the words that might be spoken of you at your funeral or memorial service. What values and traits, relationships, do you imagine your survivors sharing? Who would you like to give your eulogy? Are there things you would hope they would say? What do you need to grow into today to be worthy of these eulogies?

Prayerfully ask God to help you become the person that you hope others will see in you, your best and highest self, the person you are called to be.

Writing Your Obituary

I remember being asked to write my obituary when I was in college. I was in one of those California "touchy, feely" self-exploration classes. I don't remember exactly what I wrote, or anything about the class, except the great care our professors had for our dreams as people verging on adulthood.

Over the years, I have practiced this exercise as a way of considering my values and aspirations, the persons I sought to be and the person who made a difference to others. Our obituaries testify to the graceful and challenging interdependence of life, the reality that it takes a community to be the person you are called to be and that every life makes a difference. You can leave a mark, generate new possibilities, and provide a legacy to future generations, regardless of your social position, location, or influence. The "center is everywhere," and our calling is to bring healing, beauty, and justice to the center as it radiates beyond ourselves.

There are many ways to compose your obituary. I have witnessed poetic obituaries, taped obituaries, and paintings descriptive of a life, as well as prose obituaries. The media vary as we seek to give testimony to the life that was, the life that is, and the life that will be. Here are some ways to begin a spiritual–autobiographical obituary.

- Family of origin (parents, siblings, grandparents, important elders)
- Home and environment
- School experiences that shaped your life
- Talents and gifts
- Persons who shaped your life
- Places of education and training and their impact on your life
- Professional life and achievements
- Adult relationships
- Values and sayings you lived by
- Political and social involvements
- Retirement visions and accomplishments
- Legacy for future generations
- Words of wisdom

Imagining Death and Dying

The Greek philosopher Epicurus once noted, "If I am, death is not. If death is, I am not." While our vision of life and death may not be as stark as Epicurus', most of us are concerned with the transition from life to death. Scores of times in my pastoral ministry, congregants have told me, "I'm not afraid of death, but the dying process frightens me. I am worried about how I will die, the pain, loneliness, dependence, and diminishment." While there is much about the dying process—the cause and the timing—we cannot control, we can visualize how we might respond to the dying process.

In this spiritual exercise, visualize your last few months of life. If you have some control of the process, how would you like to die? Where would you like to spend your final days? With whom would you like to spend your last weeks, days, and hours? If you have some control of the dying process, what activities would you choose to occupy your time? While much is out of our control, what aspects of the dying process can you visualize preparing for at this time?

In the hour of death, how do you imagine your transition to the next adventure. Do you imagine nothingness, as Epicurus, or do you visualize a positive, welcoming afterlife, joining Christ "today" in paradise? In the spirit of reports of near-death experiences, do you expect anyone to greet you? Do you expect an encounter with Jesus or God? How do you understand the afterlife?

Does your vision of the afterlife shape in any way your day-to-day life? What difference does the reality of the afterlife make in your ethical, spiritual, and relational life? If there is something you are putting off till tomorrow, take time to ponder Rabbi Hillel's question, "why not now?"

From Individuality to World Loyalty

I believe, with Alfred North Whitehead, that peace of mind comes when we identify our well-being with the well-being of others, transcending the isolated, individualistic self and embracing the graceful and sometimes challenging interdependence of life. James Fowler, along with spiritual guides from all religious traditions, describes the "unitive" life as the goal of the final stages of life. We move, in this process of spiritual growth, from individual self-interest to world loyalty. We look beyond our own lives and duration on the planet to the quality of life of future generations and do our part as God's companions in healing the earth.

In this meditative exercise, I invite you set aside at least twenty minutes in a quiet, solitary environment where you are unlikely to be disturbed. Begin with simple, slow breathing, experiencing your connection with universe with each breath. With each inhaling, imagine the light of world, God's healing, connecting light, entering your whole being, body, mind, and spirit. With each exhaling, feel your connection with wider circles of relatedness. Let the circles expand larger and larger as you grow in spiritual size and impact, connecting you with:

- Your immediate physical environment.
- Your loved ones, family and friends.
- Your neighborhood and community.
- Your state, and people of diverse religious, ethnic, racial, and cultural backgrounds.
- Your nation in its diversity.
- The planet in all its wondrous human and nonhuman diversity.
- The solar system and Milky Way.
- And then finally, in the words of Buzz Lightyear from "Toy Story" to "infinity and beyond" and from time to eternity.
- As your consciousness reaches out into the unknown universe and the divinity permeating all things, begin to bring it back, circle by circle, to your own being, grateful for the interconnectedness of life, the divine energy that joins all things, and the opportunity to be a companion with God in bringing healing to the world.

As many mystics have noted, "God is a circle whose center is everywhere and whose circumference is nowhere." Wherever we are, God is the loving wisdom and energy that embraces and permeates our lives. We are safe and we are invited to grow in spiritual size to embrace life in its great abundance. In this interdependent and evolving universe, we can discover that "nothing—not even death—can separate us from the love of God."

In all of life's seasons, we can pray this. *Prayer for the Pathway: I thank you, God, for this unique, challenging, and wonderful life. Help me live gratefully and lovingly, and welcome whatever comes with courage and trust. Let me lean on your everlasting arms and from that support, reach out in love to the others. Let my living and dying glorify you and bring beauty to the world. Amen.*

NOTES

1. C. S. Lewis, *A Grief Observed* (New York: Bantam Books, 1976), 57–8.
2. Peter Koestenbaum, *The Reality of Death: Essays in Existential Psychology and Philosophy* (Westport, CT: Greenwood Press, 1971).
3. William Saroyan, *The Time of Your Life: A Comedy in Three Acts* (New York: Samuel French, 1969), 22.
4. Leslie Weatherhead was a British theologian and pastor of the City Temple in London, and author of books such as *The Christian Agnostic*, *The Will of God,* and *Life Begins at Death,* in which he considers a Christian understanding of reincarnation.
5. Real name.

Commencement Words

The Journey Ahead

I came that they might have life, and have it abundantly. (John 10:10)

With the Civil War on the horizon, Unitarian Pastor Theodore Parker proclaimed words that have echoed across the last two centuries:

> I do not pretend to understand the moral universe; the arc is a long one, my eye reaches but little ways; I cannot calculate the curve and complete the figure by the experience of sight, I can divine it by conscience. And from what I see I am sure it bends towards justice.

Virtually every pastor with whom I spoke noted the gravity of the situation that faces our nations and planet in the twenty-first century. They recognize that their days are numbered and that likelihood of them seeing 2050 is slim. Virtually all of them give thanks for the times in which we live and for their personal privilege to both enjoy and employ technology, media, travel, and medical care. Most are "numbering their days" and seeking a heart of wisdom. Yet, every pastor with whom I spoke alluded to or directly addressed their concerns for future generations in North America and across the globe. Their sense of greater unity with all life, broadening their concerns from personal and professional self-interest to world loyalty, was evident. Believing that they still have a role in creating the future, they want to be generative, to leave a mark in their immediate families, and to be forces for justice, planetary well-being, and reconciliation in the world. They want to age as they have lived, committed to God's pathway of Shalom, salvation in this life and the next.

With Theodore Parker, I believe that the universe is guided by a Divine Energy of Love, the aim toward beauty, healing, justice, and creative transformation, manifest in the prophets, wise women and men, and in Jesus of Nazareth. This Divine Wisdom and Love, embedded in the moral and spiritual arcs of history, is ubiquitous and we catch glimpses of it in every movement toward the "better angels" as well as in the teachings of the world's wisdom traditions and sages, Gautama, Lao Tzu, Mohammed, and shaman and shamanesses and spiritual guides of indigenous peoples. This belief has framed my approach to my own retirement as well as my conversations with retired clergy persons.

I believe that God is still moving in the lives of retired clergy, and that while we may be experiencing certain physical diminishments we can still be catalysts for personal and global healing. I believe that this vision is the deeper meaning of the words of 2 Corinthians (4:16–18).

> So we do not lose heart. Even though our outer nature is wasting away, our inner nature is being renewed day by day. For this slight momentary affliction is preparing us for an eternal weight of glory beyond all measure, because we look not at what can be seen but at what cannot be seen; for what can be seen is temporary, but what cannot be seen is eternal.

The pastors with whom I met know that their outer nature is or eventually will be "wasting away." Though most of them see their bodies as the temple of God and try to respond to the aging process through good health habits, they also experience the signs of gaining in daily aches and pains, medical visits, care for companions, deaths of contemporaries, and changed physical activity. Once a runner, now I walk. Once carefree in my movements, now I hold onto the rail as I go downstairs at home. I am careful when I go down the steps to the patio at night to gaze at a sky full of stars. As I write this morning, I am concerned, now that I am in a "risk" category, about the impact of the coronavirus (COVID-19) on my health. Still, we can rise like eagles and we have a job to do, a vocation for everyday and the season of retirement. Our vocation is to let go of self-interest and see the well-being of others, including species and persons we may never encounter, as important as our own. This higher love, uniting with God and creation, may begin for pastors with spouses, children and congregation, expand to grandchildren, and beyond that to other peoples' children and the future of the planet. We are, with the boy Jesus, growing in wisdom and stature. No longer needing to be conformed to the church world, we can be transformed and renewed by God's vision. (2 Corinthians 12:2)

Today's retired clergy are challenged to see themselves as images of hope. Limited in resources, not unlike our planet, we can still live abundantly and flexibly, adjusting our behaviors to be God's companions in creating a positive future for our planet. Our eschatological visions may lean toward everlasting life, but in this present moment we can be God's agents in midwifing God's realm "on earth as it is in heaven."

Retirement is the great "what's next?" for many pastors. In the years to come, we can take a well-deserved rest from professional life and intentionally adapt to aging, learning new duties for new times. We can also give thanks that God woke us up this morning to be change agents, healing the world one moment, encounter, kind word, phone call, and prophetic protest at a time.

Keeping hope won't be easy either for ourselves or for the planet. We will struggle, live through tragedy, and face uncertainty. Yet, we can become persons of large spirit, little Christs, mahatmas, and bodhisattvas, whose joy is found in growing from self-interest and self-preoccupation to world loyalty. At the end of our days, looking back on our personal and professional adventures, we will be able to affirm with Alfred North Whitehead:

> At the heart of the nature of things, there are always the dream of youth and the harvest of tragedy. The Adventure of the Universe starts with the dream and reaps tragic beauty. This is the secret of the union of Zest with Peace—that the suffering attains is end in a Harmony of Harmonies. The immediate experience of this Final Fact, with its union of Youth and Tragedy, is the sense of Peace.[1]

And with the Whitehead and Hammarskjold, we can give thanks for what has been, say yes to what will be, and commit ourselves to welcoming the great "What's next?"

A Prayer for the Pathway. Thank you, Loving Companion, for the journey of my life. Thank you for your guidance and care. Awaken me to the next steps that I might respond with grace and creativity, loving you and claiming my role as your companion in healing the world. Amen.

NOTE

1. Alfred North Whitehead, *Adventures of Ideas* (New York: Free Press, 1967), 296.

Index

About the Author

Rev. Dr. Bruce G. Epperly has served as a congregational pastor, university chaplain, professor, and seminary administrator for over forty years. He is currently Senior Pastor of South Congregational Church, United Church of Christ, Centerville, Massachusetts. He is the author of more than fifty books on practical theology, ministry, and spirituality, healing and wholeness, and process theology, including the award-winning *Tending to the Holy: The Practice of the Presence of God in Ministry*. He is also author of *A Center in the Cyclone: Twenty-first Century Clergy Self-care* and *Walking with Francis of Assisi: From Privilege to Activism*. He lives on Cape Cod, Massachusetts, with his wife Rev. Dr. Katherine Gould Epperly and near his son, daughter-in-law, and grandchildren.

Made in the USA
Monee, IL
26 July 2021

74282051R10099